Brain Friendly
School Libraries

Charles Seale-Hayne Library
University of Plymouth
(01752) 588 588

LibraryandITenquiries@plymouth.ac.uk

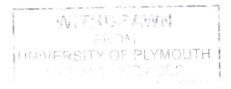

Brain Friendly School Libraries

Judith Anne Sykes

A Member of the Greenwood Publishing Group

Westport, Connecticut • London

Library of Congress Cataloging-in-Publication Data

Sykes, Judith A., 1957–
    Brain friendly school libraries / by Judith Anne Sykes.
      p. cm.
    Includes bibliographical references and index.
    ISBN 1–59158–246–6 (pbk. : alk. paper)
    1. School libraries—Aims and objectives. 2. Learning—Physiological aspects.
    3. Teacher-librarians. 4. Information literacy—Study and teaching. 5. School
    librarian participation in curriculum planning. 6. Libraries and education. 7. Brain.
    I. Title.
Z675.S3S956   2006
027.8—dc22   2005030843

British Library Cataloguing in Publication Data is available.

Library of Congress Catalog Card Number: 2005030843
ISBN: 1–59158–246–6

First published in 2006

Libraries Unlimited, 88 Post Road West, Westport, CT 06881
A Member of the Greenwood Publishing Group, Inc.
www.lu.com

Printed in the United States of America

The paper used in this book complies with the
Permanent Paper Standard issued by the National
Information Standards Organization (Z39.48–1984).

10 9 8 7 6 5 4 3 2 1

To my favourite twenty-first-century learner, my daughter Michelle

CONTENTS

PART IV GOAL 3: EMOTIONAL ENVIRONMENTS—TEACHER-LIBRARIAN
AS CULTURAL EMISSARY

FOREWORD

Education is discovering the brain and that's about the best news there
could be.... [A]nyone who does not have a thorough, holistic grasp of
the brain's architecture, purposes, and main ways of operating is as far
behind the times as an automobile designer without a full understanding of engines.

Leslie Hart, Human Brain, Human Learning
(New York: Longman, 1985)

Who is the twenty-first-century learner? The kindergarten child hugging a
treasured copy of *The Very Hungry Caterpillar*? The teenager signing out
six books and a video about the Holocaust? The first-year medical student, piled with materials on human anatomy? The auto mechanic viewing compact discs of variant engine components? The graduate education
student writing a thesis on cooperative learning? The senior citizen scan-
ning the Internet for the best travel destination? The twenty-first-century
learner is all of these people, for to learn is to continue to "grow dendrites," or build brain cells. It is what makes us human. Blockages to learning are blockages to the human experience. Learning is not "schooling"; it
is not that factory model of institutions churning out product year after
year.

Institutions, ingrained and cultural, find "change" hard to come by. Paradigms change over centuries, not overnight. The emerging twenty-first-
century learner is the learner that successful businesses and corporations
demand and describe as the independent, lifelong learner. This learner
knows how to construct knowledge from information and ideas—how to
interact with it, restructure it, create from it, communicate it, and reflect
on it. And this learner, this human being, has a brain that has evolved to
encompass these functions. When will our scholarly institutions catch up?

Libraries of all sorts, including those in schools and colleges, have long
appeared to be traditional institutions, storehouses of information, and
much of that storage primarily consists of printed books. These institutions are and have been wholly democratic—particularly public libraries
where anyone can freely borrow materials and have access to great domains of knowledge. Public libraries have experienced subliminal changes

creeping into their institutions—coffee lounges, book study groups, art displays, Internet services. Indeed, some libraries are never closed. The brain, thirsty for knowledge, will seek out information sources such as the public library or the Internet. When students aspire to learn a trade or profession, they will find that college or university libraries support them. Thus school libraries have vital roles to play in supporting learning from the day students enter as young children. School libraries not only prepare students to use future institutions, real or virtual; they can support learners throughout their schooling journey.

A city without a public library system would be unthinkable, as would a university or college without similar services, so why do the youngest brains, children in schools, not deserve the same intellectual support? As education and library service evolves over time, so must the school library move from merely providing a storehouse of materials, no matter how carefully selected and presented, to becoming a brain friendly, inviting center for constructivist learning. As educators learn more about how the brain learns and what best feeds the neural networks, they must nurture our collective intellects with renewing school libraries to become the brain friendly core of the school. Rather than storehouses of materials, there is a need to reframe the picture of the school library as a learning laboratory—where the learner's brain interacts with resources, both human and non-, and makes its own meaning and understanding of what it is the individual is studying or researching.

In this renewal process of slowly changing paradigms "teacher-librarians" are needed more than ever to fulfill an evolving and demanding role. Although documented in school library literature and graduate programs for at least twenty years, this role, practiced by many teacher-librarians, has not been practiced widely enough in some areas to preserve and grow the teacher-librarian profession. Indeed, many still wonder why a "teacher" is needed in a school library. A most thorough examination of competencies vital to this role was prepared in 1997 by the Association for Teacher-Librarianship in Canada and the Canadian School Library Association *Students' Information Literacy Needs in the 21st Century: Competencies for Teacher-Librarians.* These competencies dictate that twenty-first-century teacher-librarians be continuous learner themselves and be seen as learning leaders in schools. This necessitates understanding, expertise, and practice of current knowledge in brain research and learning, flowing into what could be considered three major areas that make them invaluable.

First is the teacher-librarian's leadership role as an *on-site staff developer.* Here is a person on a school staff who has teaching and librarian expertise and can serve as guide/mediator/facilitator for students and staff through the information age, applying best practices from brain research. To accomplish this, the teacher-librarian must see the philosophical base of his or her role as collaborative practitioner, team planner, and team teacher.

Second is the teacher-librarian's role as *information literacy agent*, planning with teachers to lead students in authentic critical inquiry through constructivist research skills and processes. And third is the teacher-librarian's role as *cultural emissary*, connecting students and staff with that latest and greatest novel, picture book, Web site, video, art print, and/or reference source.

The most important aspect of the teacher-librarian's role, and the one that needs to be articulated at every level of funding, is what it means for students. Learners from six to sixty deserve the services of a twenty-first-century teacher-librarian, who—with pedagogical knowledge of how the brain learns best—can link learners with meaningful, deep library learning experiences. Teacher-librarians are ready to make their school libraries more brain friendly and become leaders in what noted educator Pat Wolfe calls this "cognitive epoch."

PREFACE

What can a teacher-librarian learn from studying brain research? It is a question important to ask anyone in the field of education; however, owing to the vital leadership role of the twenty-first-century teacher-librarian, it is more important than ever to be aware of what scientists know about how learners learn so that the teacher-librarian can provide the resources and curriculum planning support that are key to having a successful and "in demand" brain friendly school library program.

Many educators still cling to traditional types of curriculum delivery, including the delivery of school library programs. How are information literacy skills and processes taught? Are library skills lessons being taught out of context or on an ad hoc basis using traditional teaching methods? How are students, from the youngest to the oldest, being introduced to the grand schema of culture and story that is our literature, poetry, drama, nonfictional writing, and more? This book suggests practical approaches and ideas to enable teacher-librarians to use brain compatible learning to make their school libraries and learning programs more brain friendly. Many educators are keen on what brain research is telling us but are unsure of how to approach or engage in it at the school level, including the school library. The purpose of this book is to present ways to link brain research to innovative, proven educational methods and principles.

The book was developed through the author's experience of taking graduate courses on the topic and by the application of what was learned in various ways to improve practice in the instructional leadership roles held by the author, which have been many and varied: teacher, teacher-librarian, staff developer in school libraries, assistant principal, principal, author, and presenter. Brain research findings have enabled her to change her approach to teaching as well as the work she does with staff and in conducting workshops, either slowly or rapidly introducing effective brain friendly changes into the work and inspiring others to do so as well.

There is not enough time in the day or the year to implement many of the brain friendly ideas and projects possible once an educator delves into this brave new world of neuroscience. It is hoped that teacher-librarians will take what is presented here, read up on it, apply it to suit their situations, and have another tool to transform the school library as the indispensable learning center of the school—indeed, operating in tandem the way the human brain operates, as the center for "receptivity . . . [and] information processing" (Wolfe 2001).

Admittedly, there are many cutbacks in school libraries, most ironically in this age of exploding information. In some pockets of the world, school libraries fare better than others. Studies show that having successful, appropriately staffed school library programs contributes to an increase in student achievement. If the teaching staff is operating collaboratively with the library at the center of inquiry, like the "brain," and the school library is an exciting place of authentic research, supporting learning and teaching for students and staff, a gateway to literature and the arts, it will not be seen as a "frill" or that "place down the hall to get a book for something." When dollars are tight or programs are not seen as central, they will be eliminated. But imagine a human without the brain! Or without knowledge, information processing, experiences, memory, and emotion! These are the rudimentary tools of a strong school library program—teacher-librarians need to connect with human brains to maximize learning and further intellectualize the education process.

The first part of this book presents a sampling of influential background references, outlining key concepts relating to brain research and educational practice. It includes recent Web sites that will lead the teacher-librarian into a fascinating world of science and brain friendly educational practices. It is hoped that teacher-librarians will take a further look at the subject through using the resources mentioned and others that they discover, then go on to develop ways to use them with all the learners in their school.

The author contacted three prominent educational brain research/ intelligence experts: Ellen Langer, Bob Sylwester, and Pat Wolfe. Their work is looked at more closely in additional chapters. Throughout this section of the book, suggestions are given for adapting brain research findings to teacher-librarians' work in school libraries.

The second, third, and fourth parts of this book connect three commonly occurring themes in brain-based learning that could become the primary goals for transforming a school library into a brain friendly, innovative learning center. All themes use examples that focus on the role of the teacher-librarian—the collaborative teaching partner with the teachers—in the school in supporting the curriculum and student learning. Teacher-librarians could use these concepts with their teachers to build shared understanding of brain-based learning principles and the potential for powerful school library services and programs interconnecting with the classrooms. Suggestions are given throughout for using brain friendly principles in giving workshops to the staff or in collaborative planning sessions to bring colleagues into the research and instructional planning. As teaching colleagues experience new ways of learning themselves and in working with the teacher-librarian, they will become more comfortable in using more brain friendly practices with students.

ACKNOWLEDGMENTS

I would like to acknowledge the work and words of noted brain/intelligence experts Ellen Langer, Pat Wolfe, and Robert Sylwester. Through reading and contacts with them I was able to come to a deeper understanding of what brain research could mean for school libraries.

I would like to acknowledge the Calgary Board of Education, specifically the staff, students, and families at Belfast Fine Arts/Technology Learning Centre, where I have been honoured to be their principal. The support, encouragement, and inspiration I receive on a daily basis from this learning community is invaluable. I thank them and the district for believing in my work, working with me and guiding me, supporting me to continually "think out of the box" in developing innovative schoolwide and school library learning experiences for our wonderful students.

INTRODUCTION

Picture a "brain compatible environment" as described by noted brain research educators Renate Nummela Caine and Geoffrey Caine in their book *Education on the Edge of Possibility* (1997):

> [A] large open environment for up to 150 people, working together for several hours at a stretch. In this environment everyone is a learner and both young people and adults can be facilitators.... [In] the interior landscape ... the furniture is reconfiguarable, the reference materials are delivered on demand through networked interactive multimedia, and the place is constantly buzzing with activity.... The plaza provides for videotaping on location, has the capacity to simulate physical and computer-generated models of real-world projects, and promotes the use of concept-mapping software. Works of art can be downloaded, software is available to assist in literary text analysis, and provision is made for intimate small-group discussion. The plaza is guided by a team of about five teacher facilitators who move around and maintain a big picture of what is happening with the group as a whole. (50–51)

Does this sound a little bit like the environment you work in or dream of working in day to day in your school library as you advocate to develop strong school library programs? Actually, it is a description, accompanied by an architectural sketch, of a "Creative Learning Plaza" by a company called Creative Learning Systems in California. Upon discovering it in Caine and Caine's book, the sketch looked startlingly familiar; at closer inspection I detected shelves of bookcases surrounding the "plaza." Caine and Caine go on to say that such a plaza was funded for a school project in California a few years ago. They felt that it reflected what research shows a brain-based learning environment to be with brain compatible teaching in the facilitory mode; also they thought it might be the way schools of tomorrow may be organized. They state that teachers will not be able to function in this type of environment without a radically different view of learning and teaching.

I stopped reading the book at this point, wondering if I should contact the Caines immediately to tell them these types of environments abound or have abounded in many schools in the school library or media center. Yet there is no team of "five teacher facilitators"; often there is only one—and sometimes these days not a one—called the teacher-librarian or school library media specialist, out there in that dendrite-rich learning environment, leading teachers into that "radically different view of learning and teaching."

Learning must be compatible with how the brain functions. It has just been within the last few years that neuroscience technology has advanced and is emerging so that the living brain can be studied. What is reaffirming is that brain research does validate what are considered to be the best learning and teaching practices harkening back to John Dewey and the birth of constructivism. The more educators can base their practice on what science has discovered, the less intuitive our profession becomes and the more validated are our wisest practices. What do our brains need to create the desire to learn?

Key experts in brain research (Renate Nummela and Geoffrey Caine, Eric Jensen, Pat Wolfe, Bob Sylwester) emphasize the following important modes that create optimal conditions for learning, which will be furthered explored throughout the book. You need to understand, support, lead, advocate, and be a resource for these understandings. First, the brain needs basic good health; nutrition and exercise serve as the foundation for a healthy brain. Do your staff and students know this? It really makes you question any cutbacks to physical education or health programs. We can begin to address this very simply: The brain requires regular hydration. Encourage students to bring water bottles to classes or the library, or encourage trips to the water fountain rather than not allowing students these brain-required breaks. One of my former third-grade classes was surprised to hear that just eating a bit of protein in the morning would help their concentration—peanut butter on their toast, milk, perhaps an egg. Stress active learning in brain friendly school library projects—use cooperative learning, the arts, action research, debate, and so on, as will be detailed in forthcoming chapters.

Experts go on to remind us about emotions and how they link to learning and long-term memory. Think of the key role literature and the arts play here—have not words and images from authors, poets, playwrights, and artists intertwined with peak emotional experiences most of us cannot easily forget? A humorous story? A stunning work of art? Music that stirs the soul? Another simple beginning: Try playing a variety of background music via the library's recording collection or radio to soothe or stimulate—classical, modern, jazz, baroque. Could the brain friendly school library house the student art gallery? Dramatic readings from literature?

Another area often discussed by brain research experts is the intuitive realm, where experiential and relevant learning make the strong neural connections necessary to long-term memory. Here material must have meaning to the individual studying it, or it will not remain with them. We cannot ignore or deny that we are social beings; brain research gives evidence that much of our growth also comes from working with, exploring, and talking with others. Cooperative learning strategies, students in groups, partner research—it is important to learn about these and incorporate them into collaboratively planned brain friendly school library learning experiences if they are not already a fundamental part of your school library program.

To best stimulate the brain, we must use multiple teaching and learning strategies and seize identified windows of opportunity. These windows, no matter the age or stage, are best met by focusing on the intellectual, using the processes of inquiry with which you are familiar—questioning, developing a variety of questions, hypothesizing, open-ended research assignments, problems to solve, projects in which to be immersed, critical thinking. It is crucial that you join voices with what is being said about how the brain learns with what is said about information literacy and find ways to make information literacy learning real and relevant to each individual student. The brain friendly school library must become "network central" for every classroom experience, an extension of the classroom connecting to student lives, across curricular boundaries, to other libraries, and to the community. It becomes the entity that connects and guides learning inside the school to learning outside the school and allows the world to come in—very much emulating the actual functioning of the brain.

Part I

WHAT NEUROSCIENCE TELLS US ABOUT LEARNING

Chapter 1

KEY CONCEPTS AND LITERATURE

As scientific learning advances, what we are learning about our own physiology and, in particular, our brains and how we learn is also advancing rapidly. Yet it has only been in about the last five years that we have learned almost 95 percent of what we know about the brain, owing to advanced technologies that allow neuroscientists to study the living brain. Educators find this research both exciting, budding with possibilities to transform, enhance, and impact student learning, as well as affirming, with science now validating what educators have known for years about good learning and teaching practices. The human ability and need to construct knowledge for meaning, for which our brains are hardwired, dates back to what John Dewey wrote about a century ago known as the "constructivist model of learning." This model rests on the edict that learning cannot be a prepackaged, assembly line–delivered commodity. Effective, meaningful learning experiences must be compatible with how the brain functions. To teacher-librarians, information literacy is an outcome of such opportunities for learners to put facts into construction, to work together to solve problems, and to create new understanding from the learning. The type of effective learning and teaching methods being affirmed by brain research complement and support the current literature and nationwide standards for school library practices and can lead to the transformation and renewal of school libraries.

Teacher-librarians will find much benefit to advancing their work by becoming knowledgeable practitioners with brain research tenets as the foundation to wise practice. As they become familiar with the physiological aspects of the human brain studied by neuroscience in relation to learning, the commonalities of recommended teaching principles will soon resonate with familiarity. Much of what brain research is telling us validates what we have known all along as best or wisest educational practice and what teacher-librarians have endeavoured to incorporate into collaborative planning and teaching with teachers.

There are many noted authors in the field of brain research and education. They express their findings and applications in varying amounts of detail concerning neuroscience or instructional strategy. A summary of key educators in the field of brain-based learning follows. As teacher-librarians work with teachers in attempting to use brain research to transform practice, they will discover which synthesis of brain research or which recommended practices work best for them and their teachers. Certain authors or experts in the field will become familiar or favourites in planning as they best relate to collaborative work around developing a brain friendly school library program that will impact the total school program.

Teacher-librarians will discover in the literature of brain research or brain-based learning that the teaching of curriculum needs to move from "covering it" to the meaningful concept of "uncovering" it. As the underlying structures and constructs of the great academic disciplines emerge, richer learning connections embed within long-term memory. As learning becomes more student focused, school libraries must also transform their practice from a focus on collecting and accessing materials to building centres of information exploration and creation. The teacher-librarian can take the lead in working through this developmental perspective on curriculum, to support taking students from just being exposed to learning key concepts to having them grapple with more complex conceptual systems, and disciplinary theories and guiding them in making more interdisciplinary connections. The school library with its vast interdisciplinary collection and the knowledge base of the teacher-librarian in information literacy and brain research can be instrumental in making these connections happen for students and teachers.

Where to begin? First, teacher-librarians must learn more about the brain and learning and familiarize themselves with the current national standards for school libraries that have been recently developed in both the United States and Canada. Next, teacher-librarians should make sure they are knowledgeable about their own state, provincial, or district goals and expectations for school libraries and school library personnel. These "bigger picture" standards or expectations need to be considered as teacher-librarians connect them with the principles of brain research. They will assist teacher-librarians in making the school library more brain friendly and connect their practice to what works for them. Much of what teacher-librarians will discover in brain research studies supports school library literature and research, particularly in the area of information literacy, from at least the past twenty years.

To note, from chapter 2 of *Information Power: Building Partnerships for Learning* (1998) from the American Library Association and the Association for Educational Communications and Technology, nine standards are stated to advance the development of student information literacy. These are:

Information Literacy

Standard 1: The student who is information literate accesses information efficiently and effectively.

Standard 2: The student who is information literate evaluates information critically and competently.

Standard 3: The student who is information literate uses information accurately and creatively.

Independent Learning

Standard 4: The student who is an independent learner is information literate and pursues information related to personal interests.

Standard 5: The student who is an independent learner is information literate and appreciates literature and other creative expressions of information.

Standard 6: The student who is an independent learner is information literate and strives for excellence in information seeking and knowledge generation.

Social Responsibility

Standard 7: The student who contributes positively to the learning community and to society is information literate and recognizes the importance of information to a democratic society.

Standard 8: The student who contributes positively to the learning community and to society is information literate and practices ethical behaviour in regard to information and information technology.

Standard 9: The student who contributes positively to the learning community and to society is information literate and participates effectively in groups to pursue and generate information.

Achieving Information Literacy (2003), developed by the Association for Teacher-Librarianship in Canada and the Canadian School Library Association (now the combined Canadian Association of School Libraries, or CASL), promotes a vision for twenty-first-century school libraries as "active learning laboratories." Along with this vision are standards for collections, facilities, and staffing as well as eight important student learning outcomes built around the development of information literacy. These are:

Outcome 1: Uses Information with Aesthetic Appreciation—Students will demonstrate an appreciation of the creative arts, literature, various media formats and other aesthetic representation, and the value of lifelong learning.

Outcome 2: Uses Information Responsibly—Students will use information responsibly and ethically for individual and collaborative activities.

Outcome 3: Uses Information Respectfully—Students will use information from diverse perspectives and values with respect.

Outcome 4: Uses Information Critically—Students will use information critically to evaluate the relevance, authenticity, and validity of information and its source.

Outcome 5: Uses Information Strategically—Students will use information strategically to process, organize, and select information to meet an individual or collaborative learning need.

Outcome 6: Uses Information for Decision Making—Students will consciously use information for making personal and group learning decisions.

Outcome 7: Uses Information Expressively—Students will use information expressively to modify, revise, and transform information and to communicate their newly created information with an intended audience.

Outcome 8: Uses Information and Media Tools with Technical Competence—Students will demonstrate competence and proficiency in the technical uses of traditional and digital information and media tools.

Many similar key themes from information literacy emerge over and over again in reading about brain research or brain-based learning—abilities such as:

• Accessing, evaluating, and using information (basic biological functions of the brain)
• Creativity
• Story (in its many formats that humans have technologically devised)
• Lifelong continuous learning
• Collaboration

Teacher-librarians should familiarize themselves with the key literature and authors in the field of brain research, intelligence, and education. The writing, presentations, materials, and Web sites of Geoffrey and Renate Caine, Eric Jensen, Ellen Langer, Bob Sylwester, and Pat Wolfe are most informative, influential, and useful to improving practice in collaborative learning and teaching in the brain friendly school library. Titles of professional books by these authors and others should be added to the school library's professional development section. Many conferences and workshops are also continually available relating to brain research or brain-based learning.

The works of these authors or others in the field of brain research and learning make good choices for book and/or online study groups for the teacher-librarian to sponsor and lead. Many brain research authors offer professional development videos and kits to use in working with school staffs. Often when attending sessions on brain research, presenters will design workshops using brain friendly principles in their delivery so that attendees will experience this type of learning themselves.

Each brain research expert and many of the Web sites relating to the topic discuss basic comprehension or give an introduction to the brain's

Figure 1

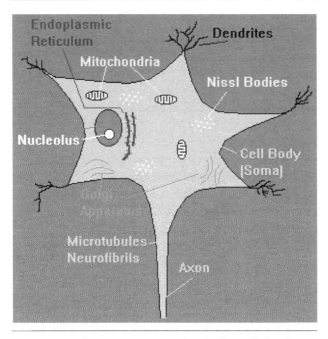

Source: http://faculty.washington.edu/chudler/cells.html

anatomy. Concisely, at the cellular level, important cells in the central nervous systems are known as "neurons." Neurons have projection-like tendrils called "dendrites" that receive information from other cells. They have a single "axon" that sends information to the other cells. Neurons communicate electrochemically by passing messages at the junction ("synapse") of the dendrite and axon. The brain adapts the neural system to our environmental demands; this plasticity is central to learning. Biologically, the neuron's structure is shown in Figure 1.

Other experts in brain research noted here and the many current Web sites available give thorough details on the biology and workings of the brain and nervous system. These can be studied, depending on the teacher-librarian's interest in the physiological information. What is important to know is that each section of the brain works together with the others to process the constant stimuli, to organize information into thought patterns, memory, and action. Interesting Web sites such as the Whole Brain Atlas (2004) (http://www.med.harvard.edu/AANLIB/home .html) allow a look at actual photographic images and video clips of all parts of the healthy brain and varied diseased conditions. Eric Chudler's Neuroscience for Kids Web site has a vast amount of student friendly information on the workings of the brain (http://faculty.washington .edu/chudler/cells.html). Depending on the reader's interests, these and other resources are often linked to the sources mentioned above to give a basic or detailed look at the biological brain. A basic understanding can help guide decisions or changes around key learning and teaching practices.

There is much excellent information available linking the scientific data to education and learning.

Renate and Geoffrey Caine's *Education on the Edge of Possibility* (1997) impacts thinking about learning and teaching in the school library owing to their encapsulation of "twelve key brain/mind learning principles" and the "Creative Learning Plaza" concept designed by Creative Learning Systems in California. The principles describe how the brain and body work together. The term "body/brain" is emerging in this literature as science enables greater understanding of the connectedness of all the systems—neural, nervous, and emotional.

The Caines relate case studies of their research in schools with recommendations about how educators need to change the way they think and teach based on what we are learning about the optimal functioning of the brain and knowledge construction. The material on the Creative Learning Centers very much resembles an active school library.

The Caines describe three instructional approaches they had observed extensively:

1. First, the traditional "stand and deliver" model (with a focus on surface knowledge).
2. Second, a form of concept teaching that is still "command and control" but uses more "complex materials" for some powerful, engaging experiences (technical or scholastic-type knowledge).
3. Third, brain-based methods where learning is student centered at its core as students "gather collectively around critical ideas, meaningful questions and purposeful projects" (dynamic knowledge).

They pose a most critical question: "How would education, including research, teaching, school buildings, administration and funding, change if we all adopted the notion of learning as the acquisition of meaningful knowledge instead of the delivery of information developed by experts?" Indeed, how would the school library space and collection and teaching practices change with this adoption?

The Caines' Web site (http://www.cainelearning.com/brain) Brain/Mind Learning details research, services, and background and gives online tools and ideas to use in the classroom that could be adapted to the school library program and be promoted in collaborative learning and teaching experiences. The site also includes a manageable few but important links to other pertinent resources such as a literature Web site that connects to a government site (that does include school libraries), two unique school programs to view founded on brain principles, and the Creative Learning Systems (2004) site (http://www.clsinc.com).

On this site the Creative Learning Plaza operating in a California secondary school is featured. The theory and what the students are doing in this school emulate the loftiest goals of the American and Canadian School Library Association Standards. The plaza is described as the "ultimate in collaborative learning" and has secondary students (grades nine through twelve) in various high-tech "centers" or "stations" simultaneously: gathering digital images to use in a newsletter, brainstorming about computer coding changes to a robot they programmed, or videoconferencing with a grad student at a university across the country as they work in small groups surrounded by resources and guided by teachers or other mentors, in real and/or virtual time.

The Caines' Web site also provides the list of their twelve brain/mind learning principles (first published in 1989); they give one another way of articulating what brain research is telling us is critical to learning and teaching.

Eric Jensen's books (1995, 1996) and Web site (2004) (http://jlcbrain .com/main.html) are other useful sources. The Web site is from the Jensen Learning Corporation (formerly Turning Point) and is a professional training organization founded by Diane and Eric Jensen. Diane was a former Teacher of the Year, and Eric Jensen was the co-founder of the world's first and largest brain compatible teen program (SuperCamp) in 1982. He is a well-known presenter and author in the field of brain research and education. At the site is information and registration forms for Jensen-directed brain research conferences and workshops, including a rigorous certification program. There is an online newsletter (*The Brain Store News Service*) and recommended Web sites along with a quick quiz on brain research, which would be useful to start a discussion. Another good discussion starter would be the Web site article "Brain-Based Learning, Truth or Deception" that critically looks at the myths and applications of using brain research in educational practice. There is a "Brain Store" online where many additional resources may be ordered.

One of Jensen's books, *The Learning Brain* (1995), introduces the very complex concepts of brain research in an easily digestible presentation. Over 300 pieces of research are presented but are synthesised into one- to two-page notations that include the research summary, examples, implications to learners, action steps educators can implement immediately, and where warranted, recommended further reading. The teacher-librarian can use this resource to learn much of the basics and background in brain research and application and to browse, read, and use sections that are of particular interest or demand. The teacher-librarian may find that knowing about learning environments is important in the actual setup and design of a brain friendly school library when Jensen addresses topics such as research on "Enriched Environments Build Better Brains." He cites the important research of scientist Dr. Marian Diamond at Berkeley and under "Actions" recommends creating a more multisensory environment with posters, music, aromas, more engaging and relevant activities, different rooms, larger areas, and changing environment to create novelty and challenge to allow students to practise critical skills such as categorising, counting, labeling, language, cause and effect, and thinking.

In *Brain-Based Learning* (1996), Jensen goes into further detail on twenty-three topics relating to brain research and learning. This book is again a very comprehensive and easily digestible source to assist in making changes in practice; it also works well as a reference book. For example, the chapter "Brain-Based Environments" gives the teacher-librarian references for attending to the physical space. Boxes indicating "What This Means to You" follow short discussions of theory and research. In the entry on "lighting," it suggests soft, natural lighting; a variety of lighting; and giving learners choice and change in where they sit. Thus, seating could be rearranged, window coverings removed, and bright, inviting separate workspaces created for students in the school library.

Another very comprehensive source is the second edition of *The Owner's Manual for the Brain* by Pierce J. Howard (2000). At first this tome appears intimidating at over 800 pages, but it is truly an interesting read or reference source, indeed, it is a very practical guide on everything to know about the brain from the biology and science (in very readable terms) to lengthy, informative sections on health, gender differences, illness, emotion and learning, attention, and memory. Similar to Jensen's work, each topic such as "Practice" is given a short explanation of the research, followed by a list of practical tips called "applications."

A study of the brain also involves a deeper look at memory. "The only evidence we have of learning is memory," states Marilee Sprenger in her book *Learning and Memory: The Brain in Action* (1999). Sprenger is a middle school teacher from Illinois who leads workshops and training sessions in brain compatible teaching and learning. Reinforcing the concepts that "social interaction, care, challenge and play" grow dendrites, Sprenger reminds educators to aim for lots of positive feedback, teaming, and movement in planning learning experiences for students, stimulating the release of positive chemical reactions in the brain. This type of learning prevailing in a school library may be dramatically different than traditionally practised.

Sprenger's book is an easily read, fascinating entry into brain biology, chemistry, and memory as she uses many daily and practical examples and ideas to create meaning around the content. Beginning with the cellular level of the brain, she delves into the chemistry of the brain's workings in an interesting section that gives greater insight into human behaviour. Sprenger proceeds to explain five types of known memory inherent in the brain. Learning about these helps educators know how and when to pause and examine what they are seeking to teach and what might be the best way to reach that goal and impact all the types of "memory lanes":

• Semantic (word memory of an event/learning experience)
• Emotional (feelings at the time of event/learning)
• Automatic (conditioned response memory to event/learning)
• Episodic (location-oriented memory of the event/learning)
• Procedural (movements occurring during the event/learning)

Sprenger informs us that memories are what help us make decisions, affect our actions and reactions, and determine our courses in life. When more than one type of memory is accessed, the memory thus becomes more powerful. Teaching to multiple memory lanes makes connections to learning experiences stronger and easier to access. Sprenger makes suggestions to teach to each type of memory. For example, semantic memory is strengthened by "chunking" learning with strategies used in information literacy literature such as graphic organizers, peer teaching, questioning strategies, summarizing, role-playing, debates, outlining, time-lines, and paraphrasing. Procedural memory thrives on movement and repetition; Sprenger advises us to take breaks often, change activities, and engage in physical movement. For automatic, emotional memory, she suggests putting learning to music or having students create a quiz show. Sprenger suggests that making learning experiences unique may make them permanent in memory—for example, field trips or library learning experiences! All types of memory are brought into play through two key areas the teacher-librarian can influence—storytelling and research processes. These are very good for the brain and memory.

In the information age there is an abundance of material on this fascinating, important topic of brain research and education. In addition to the Web sites already mentioned, three additional Internet sites merit mention. The Brain Connection (2004) site (http://www.brainconnection .com) has a very comprehensive library with many links to current information on the brain and its applications to education along with the usual resources and conferences available. It has "brain teaser" activities for children and a section devoted to the "Education Connection—Applying Brain Science to Learning and Teaching." In this section there is a regular column written by noted expert Bob Sylwester, who is included in chapter 3 of this book as a primary source. The July 2004 column, titled "The Deep Roots of the Arts," delves into Sylwester's support of this vital aspect of education. Links to other sources on the arts and the brain are featured with Sylwester's article. The arts prove to be a vital component in brain-based learning and will prove to be in brain friendly school libraries.

It is interesting to note in the May 2004 report on "The Arts in Ontario's Public Schools" that pages nine through eleven are devoted to "School Libraries and the Arts." This report, from People for Education in Ontario, Canada, was commissioned by a group of parents working for public education improvement in that province. This section of the report addresses the crisis they discovered in Canadian school library staffing and children's book publishing but goes on to state a school library's importance to the arts in that "school libraries and teacher-librarians may introduce students to their first [Canadian] novels. They expose students to non-fiction books and materials, works on music, theatre and dance" (11).

The noted Dana Alliance for Brain Initiatives (2004) also advocates for the arts and brain-based learning (http://www.dana.org). Here is a gateway to the latest research on the human brain. The site is organized into three sections—brain centre, immunology (news and research on the immune system), and arts education. As stated on the site, "The Dana Foundation is a private philanthropic organization with particular interests in neuroscience, immunology, and arts education." Dana Alliance for Brain Initiatives is a nonprofit organization of more than 200 preeminent neuroscientists, including ten Nobel laureates, and is dedicated to advancing education about the brain. The "Arts Education" initiative at Dana supports innovative programs leading to improved teaching in the performing arts in public schools. Grants, guidelines, publications, and resources are all here online, as are many free Dana Press publications and newsletters.

Dee Dickinson's Web site New Horizons for Learning (http://www .newhorizons.org) is the site of the company of the same name founded in 1980 with long service as a leading-edge resource for educational change through its online journal, books, and other written materials; networking people and organizations; and international conferences. Included on this site are articles, recommended readings, and links to the latest in neuroscience. Other sections have excellent articles, links, and recommended readings on the topics of transforming education, perspectives on the future, special needs, and student voices. A section on lifelong learning has much information on adult learning and would be useful to the teacher-librarian in collaborative planning or conducting workshops. "Teaching and Learning Strategies" addresses many brain friendly techniques that will be discussed in forthcoming chapters of this book, such as action research, arts in education, assessment alternatives, cooperative learning, democratic classrooms, emotional intelligence, environments for learning, graphic tools, learning styles, literacy, multiple intelligences, technology in education, thinking skills, and more.

There is no end to information at our fingertips today on any topic, and brain research is no different. The teacher-librarian will want to do some background work; discover favourite, noted authors or Web sites; and experiment with implementing changes in practice or new ideas from this book or others in collaboration with teachers. The next three chapters present detailed views on brain research, learning, and the school library from Ellen Langer, Bob Sylwester, and Pat Wolfe, followed by sections on practical ideas the teacher-librarian can use in the school library framed around brain friendly practices.

Chapter 2

ELLEN LANGER—MINDFUL LEARNING

Ellen Langer provides insight into the area of intelligence that the teacher-librarian can apply to further impacting brain friendly school library practices. As documented in her book *The Power of Mindful Learning* (1997), Langer, a professor of psychology at Harvard University, has received numerous awards including the Guggenheim Fellowship for this groundbreaking work in intelligence theory conducted around many educational trials. One of the major messages Langer urges educators to adhere to is to move away from rote learning and the traditional concept of finding "right answers" to the realization of awareness of context and the ever-changing nature of information. This reinforces the principles of brain-based learning and forms the basis of what school library literature paints as the information literate learner.

Langer clarifies what we traditionally think of as "intelligence" and mindfulness in the following ways. Intelligence traditionally is seen as a fit between the individual and environment. It is linear, outcome based, and from the observer's perspective. It has stable categories, remembered facts, and learned skills in context. Mindfulness comes at reality from several perspectives—stepping back from perceived problems or solutions to view them as new, giving meaning to outcomes, developing personal control by shifting perspectives, and depending on the fluidity of knowledge and skills and recognizing the advantages and disadvantages in each.

The standards of information literacy fall heavily into this category of mindfulness. This premise should be familiar to teacher-librarians through information literacy literature. In this century more than at any other time, libraries are key in the role they play in a world of ever-changing information. Libraries, and librarians, provide access to information, organize it, and carefully select and analyse it. The school library has a central role and focus to prepare students to be able to deal with information in all formats and become lifelong learners and critical thinkers, understanding bias and many points of view. Langer warns about "debilitating myths" about lifelong learning such as aging. She views this as a stereotype fallen into due to conditioning and cultural memory, which schools are a part of perpetuating. There is no reason to ever stop learning.

Additionally, Langer addresses intelligence in a broader sense and finds that her research shows that intelligence cannot be easily categorized as "multiple" or "emotional" in a sense that infers that some individuals have more of one type of intelligence than others. This is a shift in thinking in intelligence theories but makes perfect sense in the teacher-librarian's work in information literacy, as Langer sees a person's ability to demonstrate various talents or intelligences as largely contextual, dependent on the situation and the premise that people are taught how to live in "worlds of multiple perspectives." By preparing students to be critical thinkers and producers of information in a variety of ways in the development of information literacy, the teacher-librarian prepares them to practise and develop perspective and intelligence in many varied ways. Langer compares this to how actors prepare for various roles when they study and analyse a variety of characters and situations.

A good example of this from Langer's research is a case cited with medical students. So much of their studies in the area of disease had been based on rote memory work, which many of the medical students found explicitly boring and dreaded. One group was taught in a different way— to present the study of disease as a role-play. Students were told to role-play that they actually had the disease they were studying and to learn as much about it as they could. This "mindful" learning made a significant difference in the enjoyment of the students' learning of the subject as well as raising their achievement scores and comprehension.

Langer and others state that rote practice equals boredom; and in a telephone conversation with me, she poses the question for teacher-librarians to think about their own learning experiences and how they learned best. The teacher-librarian has an opportunity as a specialist in the school to initiate change applied to teaching methodology and to model this change in collaborative work. Langer is positive about the teacher-librarian's role of teaching students to enjoy excellent literature or to become adept researchers. The practice, though, must move from rote practices—such as "memorizing the Dewey decimals"—to relevant learning where students can become authentic, constructivist researchers with a passion to know the content.

Langer goes on to say that in the realm of fiction, fiction must be related or connected to the lives of the students, whether a modern novel, picture book, or Shakespearean play. With new knowledge that can rapidly change former knowledge, Langer states that nonfiction works can often be disputed. She views fiction and nonfiction as merging fields. What is fiction today may not be fiction some day, and vice versa, so it is not enough to try to have relevant materials in a library to interest students; the teacher-librarian must understand the individual the students bring to us. Through brain friendly school library experiences and projects, the teacher-librarian needs to prepare the students to know how to make material meaningful to them as unique individuals, to connect it to their experiences or lives.

Students need to understand that by understanding how a library is organized, they are opening themselves to a range of interdisciplinary connections as they read or conduct research. Langer emphasizes the importance of questions, of the inquiry process. Questions increase the power of mindful learning and form the basis of constructivist research. Further, Langer reminds the teacher-librarian not to attempt to make the best choice from among available options but to create options. A brain friendly school library program must allow students the opportunity to produce original thinking and materials from their research in many different ways—from painting storyboards of favourite books to building Web sites of their own research projects. Langer has found that often libraries are poor examples of mindful learning because the categorization of everything appears rigid. Students must learn that knowledge is much more interconnected, belonging to and connecting in many "sections" or fields. She feels that the role of teacher-librarian would be much more interesting if the teacher-librarian incorporates the many ways books and other resources are used and can connect in an interdisciplinary fashion. Langer emphasises that this would make the role of the teacher-librarian increase in importance. Langer gives the example at a college level of an architect student looking for resources—the architect student needs not only the architectural section of the library but style, the arts, and other areas. Librarians are thus advised to practise the art of generative questioning with diverse questions such as how a "concrete building" might relate to another area such as "cooking."

Langer has sensed that many librarians seem slow to change as if the categories in the library "wag the dog"—not the other way around. Therefore the challenge in the school library is to incorporate mindful learning into the collaborative planning and teaching process of the brain friendly school library. With some teachers this will be welcomed; with others it will take time. With all, it will take careful study of learning more about current findings in intelligence and brain research to best plan brain friendly learning experiences for the students.

Chapter 3

BOB SYLWESTER—APPLYING BIOLOGICAL RESEARCH

Robert Sylwester, emeritus professor of education at the University of Oregon, is a noted expert in the field of brain research and education. His focus relies heavily on the educational implications of new developments in science and technology, and he has written several books and many journal articles and has given countless conference and in-service presentations about brain research and education. The author of *A Biological Brain in a Cultural Classroom: Enhancing Cognitive and Social Development Through Collaborative Classroom Management* (2003), Sylwester's work is extremely informative in helping educators understand and connect neuroscience with educational practice. Sylwester poses thought-provoking inquiry and discussion questions that could spark much authentic dialogue between teacher-librarians and teachers in collaborative planning sessions.

In *A Biological Brain in a Cultural Classroom* (2000), Sylwester asks educators to contemplate substantial cuts to educational arts programs; we should also contemplate the effect of funding reductions to school libraries. With the arts programs, he asks educators to ponder what the cuts have done to the many students leaving school as non–arts grads since trained arts teachers were often eliminated in tough budgetary times. Will these students understand the importance of aesthetics in their future worlds? What kind of society does this make? The same question can be posed around school libraries, which also resource and support arts programs, as well as all the other subjects and programs in a school. What about the many students leaving schools who are not grounded in information literacy because teacher-librarians have been eliminated in budget cutting? How will these students cope with today's mass media and information overflow? How will they cope with research work in postgraduate settings? What kind of society does this make?

According to the work substantiated by Daniel Goleman (*Emotional Intelligence: Why It Can Matter More Than IQ* [1995]), the best access to weak factual memories is through strong emotional memories. This is why the humanities and the arts are basic to education. Emotion and attention are the gateways to learning and memory in a brain friendly environment; and Sylwester states the importance of "story" (arts, culture, humanities, literature, history, and so on) as linking memory and emotion.

Sylwester makes an analogy comparing how the brain functions with a model of a library or librarian.

> Our brain has an arousal system (EMOTION) to alert us to potentially important challenges, a focusing system (ATTENTION) to quickly direct us to the key elements of the challenge—separating the currently important (foreground) from the currently unimportant (background), a storage and retrieval system (MEMORY) to provide supportive information from past experience, a solution system (PROBLEM SOLVING) to determine how best to respond to the current challenge, and a motor system (BEHAVIOR) that executes our response. It's an evolved set of systems that functions efficiently. It seems to me that this also describes the organization of a library, a sort of technological extension of our brain.
>
> So librarians might consider brain/library analogies: a reception area that alerts patrons to new books and special areas of library focus, an electronic card catalog that efficiently allows patrons to focus on and locate the in-library and Internet information they need, a well-organized appropriate materials collection that patrons can easily use, and tables/word processors/etc. that patrons can use to assemble library information into assigned reports. Our brain also just muses about things without any goal in mind and a library similarly should be arranged for browsing. (Sylwester 2000, 11, and personal communication)

Sylwester continues on to say that a twenty-first-century school library should be providing current nontechnical information about cognitive neuroscience developments at a level suitable for patrons. "Brain books that were published ten plus years ago are probably out of date" (ibid.).

Sylwester's newest book is *How to Explain a Brain: An Educator's Handbook of Brain Terms and Cognitive Processes* (2004). It consists of basic encyclopaedic explanations and discussions of 280 brain terms and cognitive processes that educators are increasingly confronting and are not sure they completely understand. It is perhaps the kind of nontechnical reference book that a school library would find very useful. As mentioned earlier in this book, Sylwester writes a current monthly column (archived) on the Brain Connection Web site (http://www.brainconnection.com). This archived column addresses many timely and topical issues, and the articles could be used to facilitate professional dialogue when teacher-librarians are planning and working with teachers.

In a question posed to Sylwester via email interview, in June 2004, he thought that there might be impediments facing school librarians in using brain research to change traditional practices.

> School librarians might find that developing and maintaining a current appropriate collection is certainly a problem for librarians who don't

themselves understand brain biology. Cost is an impediment. A typical librarian's orientation toward print materials (such as encyclopaedias) in an era in which students typically search for information online might be an impediment. When students gather information from print journal/book sources, they can be pretty sure that the material has been checked for validity and accuracy, because credibility is important if it's expensive to print/distribute something. Since it's relatively easy to put something on the Internet, students now have to develop skills to check the credibility of the sources they use.... [T]eaching online research skills is certainly a central challenge. (Personal communication)

In *A Celebration of Neurons* (1995), Sylwester presented the concept of a modular brain around the librarian/library model of our brain's organization and operation. In this writing, he extends the metaphor of how the brain carries out many of the same information functions for our body that a librarian and library materials carry out for a school. Neural networks can be thought of as similar to books, except that it must be remembered that books are passive in their reception of printed material, whereas neurons in a network actively participate in the processing of information. A chemical net opens and closes to increase and decrease information flow in and out of the brain; in library budgets, patron demographics and checkout procedures help determine and regulate what enters and leaves a library. Relating to memory: The "amygdala and hippocampus" parts of the brain process the same kinds of selection and classification tasks with memories that a librarian performs with books and other materials. A librarian, with input from staff and students, selects materials to add to the library collection, just as the amygdala selects experiences for long-term memory. The hippocampus stores memory like a card catalogue, while the "cortex receives, categorizes, and interprets sensory information, makes rational decisions, and activates behavioural responses like the library building stores and retrieves memories that represent the objects and events of the external world similar to sections of the library" (41–49). A school library can function like the "central brain" of a school.

Sylwester advocates highly regarding the importance of technology in education: He writes that now thirty-five years have passed since word processors came into their own. All businesses are now computer-driven, but he reiterates in his writing that education is still pencil-driven. This is still true in many cases in 2006. Some teachers will revert to the argument that especially younger pupils do not have the dexterity or development to use computers instead of pencils. Sylwester demonstrates through research cited that the brain enables students to learn touch-typing early as well as cursive. Schools are more than a few steps behind the technologies that define our culture. Instead of having student brains exploring concepts, creating metaphors, estimating, predicting, cooperating on group tasks, or discussing moral or ethical issues, processes reflective of the standards of information literacy, schools are still doing what brains do not enjoy, such as using textbooks that compress content, writing and rewriting reports, completing repetitive worksheets, and memorizing facts that can be considered irrelevant. As Sylwester (1995) says: "Doing worksheets in school prepares a student emotionally to do worksheets in life," giving them little "cognitive challenge" (77). This can be especially challenging for teacher-librarians in collaborative planning with teachers who take a narrow pedagogical point of view.

Sylwester suggests that schools should concentrate more on developing student's ability to quickly locate, estimate, organize, and interpret information, using the superior speed and accuracy of available information technologies whenever a complex problem requires an accurate solution. This assists the student's potential understanding of the nature of computerized information and the social, political, and ethical issues that computers create. Students lack the ability to differentiate sense from nonsense in mass media. Sylwester's statements reflect the standards of information literacy.

Sylwester (2003) discusses how the brain solves problems, and he also looks at intelligence, specifically Gardner's multiple intelligences theory (82–83). Sylwester sees Gardner's work (1983) as groundbreaking owing to its expanding view of intelligence. He divides Gardner's intelligences into three sections that define human activity: time and sequence, space and place, personal and social awareness. He feels that humans develop each form of intelligence to basic functional levels in problem solving innately and through experience. Therefore, there is power in both individual learning and cooperative behaviour in a diverse society; the brain is designed for cooperative activity. Too often schools resort to making too much of individual performance and achievements rather than using the principles of cooperative learning, planning, and teaching.

Cooperative learning is a critically important aspect of school library program success for student learning and will be addressed in a further chapter in this book. Sylwester states the students must help create and directly interact with their learning through projects, cooperative learning (the grouped class as "social brain"), portfolio-type assessments—these methods place the student at the centre of the education process and thus stimulate greater learning. Sylwester (1995) also reminds readers of the importance of positive human interaction using Marion Diamond's words (133). The famous neuroscientist experimented with laboratory animals; she treated her animals (rats) well, and they did well—those treated with "tender loving care."

Sylwester writes that education is or should be at the edge of a major transformation. Another metaphor he uses to describe the brain is an evolutionary, junglelike organism, a better metaphor than the common one comparing the brain to a computer, which is highly inaccurate biologically. Educators must enter into the process of learning about the brain and the educational applications now, or biologists may well redefine our profession. Education has been likened to a "folklore" profession but can now move into science—Sylwester notes that once medicine was also a folklore profession.

Education is also a politically driven system, and it needs to move away from politics to a scientifically driven profession. Sylwester (1995) says that students' "genes" and the home environments that they come to us with cannot be altered; but school experiences that enhance the development of students' brains can be implemented by moving away from "pencil-driven, sedentary environments that are not biologically mobile classrooms." Students will resist programs that are not in tune with their "cognitive rhythms." "The fewer opportunities young people have to succeed in mainstream society and the classroom, the more social instability we can expect," Sylwester argues. He states that the classroom—and that would extend to the school library—should be viewed as a learning "laboratory" where students must *first* learn how to solve problems in their own limited worlds in democratic environments before they can help solve global problems (85).

.

Chapter 4

PAT WOLFE—BRAIN RESEARCH AND CLASSROOM PRACTICE

Patricia Wolfe is one of the leading experts on understanding brain research and on how to use this growing body of information to advance educational practice. She has been a teacher and a staff developer and now, as an independent consultant, gives presentations and workshops about using brain research in educational practice. Her teachings are also available to us in her writing, on her professional development tapes, and on her Web site (http://www.patwolfe.com).

In a personal communication with her in June 2004, Wolfe would advise teacher-librarians, as she would all teachers, that when they are exploring and implementing brain research, they will need to become very strategic in understanding what that research reports. They should endeavor to understand the rationale behind the scientific data first, then put it into practice by applying brain friendly strategies. It seems as though educators are often caught in the paradigm of teaching the way they were taught. Educators need to connect with what students store in their minds. Much of what brain research is validating is effective teaching practice. Effective teaching practice is important for teacher-librarians to have studied in order to be able to suggest and model when using collaborative planning and teaching processes.

Wolfe's work is encouraging and motivating for teacher-librarians who wish to follow the developments of brain research and to begin to change aspects of their practice and leadership. Wolfe's book *Brain Matters: Translating Research into Classroom Practice* (2001) is a wonderful choice for teacher-librarians leading a teacher book study group. Wolfe's clear, thoughtful, and practical prose takes the reader through the biology of the brain into the practical educational applications. Each chapter concludes with inquiry questions that an individual or group could use to further understand and apply the chapter contents.

Wolfe begins with thorough documentation, including many diagrams that bring the inner world of neurons, dendrites, and the physical structure of the brain into focus. She writes that the more that is understood about the brain, the better instruction will be able to be designed to match how the brain learns best. Wolfe worries that some educators might approach the subject cynically as another educational "bandwagon": "[W]e did brain-research last year, what's new this year?" (V). Wolfe states that time must be taken to look at research critically. With that critical eye it becomes apparent in many circumstances that education now has scientific data to back up classroom activities. It is up to teacher-librarians to decide how to use this research to best inform their practice because the more they understand the functioning of the brain, the better they can match instruction to address the diversity of the classrooms they serve. Teacher-librarians would find themselves more able to develop successful teaching practices for those with attention deficit hyperactivity disorder (ADHD), dyslexia, autism, and other problems that affect student performance. In the expected leadership role of teacher-librarians, they will need to be able to discuss this research with teachers, administrators, and parents as practices in their work change and develop.

Wolfe states that our understanding of what we read and hear depends largely on context. Contrary to right brain/left brain theories, biologically, both halves of the brain work together, so experiential learning must be designed to teach to both. Content in context must be meaningful to the student, and the student must grasp how it can be used in his or her own life. When planning projects with teachers, teacher-librarians need to ask how what they are teaching fits into the "big picture." What is the student's realm of application of this knowledge? Often when schools are continually faced with standardized testing, teachers argue that they must "cover" overloaded curriculum. Instead of "coverage," Wolfe (2001) states that what is needed is "to teach a lot less a lot better" (129). Wolfe discusses that the duration of information memory and understanding increases by working with it, which she refers to as "rehearsal" or practice, a key with teacher or teacher-librarian in the role of facilitator or guide. Thus students are doing most of the work themselves, as opposed to having their minds wander in lecture-type situations. This "learning by doing" consolidates memory.

Wolfe discusses the need for enriched environments for both students and teachers. A brain friendly classroom—or library—has a climate that allows students to naturally increase the pleasure factors in the brain, making the educational experience more pleasurable and rewarding, which leads to deeper learning and embedding of the learning in long-term memory. The brain must filter the enormous amount of information entering the senses: How does it determine what is relative to store in there and what is not? Wolfe states that our species has not survived by attending to and storing meaningless information but wonders if that is what schools teach and why student brains often refuse to attend.

The brain thrives on "novelty, intensity and movement" in initially attending to stimuli. Many educators use motivational techniques to garner attention. Eventually, Wolfe says, the process of "habituation" occurs, and the brain tunes the novelty out. Embedding learning within long-term memory requires sustaining attention by getting at meaning and emotion. Wolfe stresses emotion as a key factor in learning, and employing it in instructional design must be planned in "emotionally healthy" ways. Teacher-librarians are wise to recall which of their own school experiences stand out. Those that stand out will have had an emotional component. And, yes, some of those may not have been all that healthy!

Wolfe gives many practical suggestions teacher-librarians can adapt to their work immediately. They can make use of analogies, similes, metaphors, and mnemonics to make meaning from associations—for example, the mnemonic "Every good boy deserves favour" for learning the musical scale. In learning basic research skills, such as resource location, students could create, with teacher and teacher-librarian facilitation, a mnemonic to help them learn Dewey by using the first letters of each Dewey section and finding a resource from the section that sparks their interest to create an interesting mnemonic.

Wolfe discusses problem- and project-based learning, which are well suited to the collaborative teaching and brain friendly school library program. It is important, she states, that students solve real problems and use role-play in tackling curricular concepts. She suggests examples at every grade level, such as letting elementary students set up a grocery store to learn basic math instead of giving them a worksheet. Teacher-librarians must extend thinking around realism in planning for learning, such as using action research methodology where students develop questions and hypotheses around the content they are studying. Instead of researching animals, have them develop a question about the animal, its purpose, or ecological status or connection to people. For additional ideas, Wolfe reminds us that there are many "problem-based learning" and project-based books and Internet sites available. When using problems or projects repeatedly, it is important to remember to change a variable or set up another similar situation another time so students can transfer learning to a bigger picture and see connections.

A critical point, Wolfe relates, is that learning is ultimately more beneficial when students themselves create the project. For example, they could make a music video based on a novel they have been reading that the teacher-librarian and the English teacher worked together to facilitate. Projects include a variety of brain friendly components in steps along the way, such as organization of the project where graphic organizers (mind maps) set out to organize information. Graphic organizers resemble the structure used by the brain to organize information. Storyboarding or plot graphs relate to the visual/auditory senses. Much of the success in writing or developing a project depends on what has occurred before the student actually starts.

Wolfe's Web site would make a viable introduction to an online study group. Wolfe lists the most current books and Web sites she recommends for up-to-date information on brain research. Her newest book, titled *Building the Reading Brain* (with Pat Nevills; 2004), should highly interest

teacher-librarians. The Web site also details when and where Wolfe is doing workshops or presentations and lists other presenters or events she
recommends.

The Web site (see Wolfe 2004) includes three timely articles by Wolfe:
"The Adolescent Brain: A Work in Progress," "Brain Research and Education: Fad or Foundation?" and "It's All Academic: A Few Thoughts on
Brain Development in the Early Years"—all with additional recommended readings. Wolfe provides an alphabetical list, continually updated,
of articles available on various topics relating to brain research, such as
"Action Research" from *Educational Leadership* (March 2002). Also provided is "Pat Wolfe's Annotated Bibliography of Books on the Brain,"
books on disorders such as ADHD, and additional audiovisual resources.
Finally, Wolfe provides us with a comprehensive list of links to explore
brain research and education further. Teacher-librarians will find this site
extremely useful in the study of the topic.

Chapter 5

CREATING A BRAIN FRIENDLY
SCHOOL LIBRARY PLAN

The best way to move forward with applying brain research to the school library program is to create a brain friendly school library plan. In this plan the teacher-librarian will need to formulate brain friendly school library goals around the key themes or concepts that arise throughout the literature pertaining to brain research and human intelligence. In the ensuing three sections of this book, a framework of goals and strategies focusing on three major areas of brain research is suggested and linked to three key roles of the teacher librarian:

- Staff developer
- Information literacy "agent"
- Cultural emissary (literature and the arts)

Brain friendly school library goals could be part of a teacher-librarian's general overall school library plan, the plan that encompasses the collection development policy, budget, goals, and so on. This plan needs to be articulated yearly with the staff, and strategies to achieve brain friendly school library goals need to be part of the larger "school improvement" or "school development plan." All school districts require schools to have growth, development, or improvement plans, and in most schools, staff are involved in one way or another. The trend in most districts is for maximum staff collaboration around the school growth plan—the school's vision, mission, purpose, and the learning goals to improve student achievement. The teacher-librarian needs to be involved as much as possible in this process. If there is a school development committee or work group in your school, the teacher-librarian is wise to volunteer for this or request membership. If uncertain about how the process works in a particular school, the teacher-librarian should meet with the principal and open the discussion. Let the principal know about the research on the brain and learning and your ideas for impacting student learning through developing a more brain friendly school library.

During the school development planning process, the teacher-librarian has the opportunity to collaborate with the teachers, department heads, and administrators to weave goals related to developing a brain friendly school library through staff development, information literacy, and cultural literacy. The teacher-librarian can get an idea as to how the goals of developing a brain friendly school library can fit with the larger goals of the school. Perhaps the school is already focusing on brain research, or perhaps the teacher-librarian will be the catalyst to introduce it. Most school development plans have a goal around literacy, usually the traditional goal of getting students to read more or produce better reading scores. In the teacher-librarian's role as staff developer, a book study could be organized using Pat Wolfe's new book *Building the Reading Brain* (Wolfe and Nevills 2004). The teacher-librarian could suggest working with each English teacher on one brain friendly book project this term or working with each science teacher on one of his or her units this year to have students do brain friendly action research projects.

As the teacher-librarian works with the staff, they will discover the timing and connections to plan brain friendly library learning experiences that meet the readiness of the group. Prior to school improvement or individual collaborative planning sessions, the teacher-librarian needs to have prepared a draft copy of the brain friendly school library plan. The teacher-librarian's background knowledge and goals need to be drafted so that he or she can use his or her burgeoning knowledge of brain research and brain friendly educational practices with the larger staff in preparation for working with all the classes and teachers. When the staff has settled on school development goals for the year, the teacher-librarian will need to revisit the school library plan draft in order to revise as indicated. Some schools will leap ahead in embracing brain research and educational changes, particularly if teachers can work with a teacher-librarian and experiment with new ideas in the school library environment. Others may need more time, to start slowly or to observe changes, so the teacher-librarian's timelines may need adjustment, such as working with two English teachers on a brain friendly book project if not all five teachers are ready.

When the teacher-librarian is ready with the draft of a brain friendly school library plan and goals for the year, it needs to be shared with the staff, highlighting areas of importance. This may be best accomplished by meeting with the principal to present the draft and discuss the best way to share it with the staff. Usually there is an opportunity at the beginning of the school year for the teacher-librarian to remind teachers about library procedures, student orientations, equipment sign-out, and so forth. Changes or modifications to these standard areas may arise due to adopting more brain friendly practices. Initially, the staff may not be too interested in collection development plans or the like, but the teacher-librarian needs to advocate the importance of involving them, as the school library—collection and all—moves into a greater brain friendly mode. The teacher-librarian needs to take the time to share the school library goals with them for feedback and discussion, goals that should show how the school library program intertwines with the classrooms and the larger goals of the school. Discussion may follow, or teachers may take the information to be digested later; therefore, a copy of the school library plan should be made available to all. If the school has a "school handbook," this would be a good place for the plan, making sure it is updated annually.

When writing the draft of a brain friendly school library plan, it is a good idea to organize it into sections, such as those recommended in many school library resources. Generally, the teacher-librarian will:

- Reflect on the makeup of the school.
- Suggest goals for a (brain friendly) school library and how they might be achieved.
- State school library policies and a collection development plan.
- Develop brain friendly student learning outcomes for the school.

THE SCHOOL

Beginning with a brief description of the school and its programs, the teacher-librarian needs to explore the readiness of the school—students, staff, leadership, and parents—to accept brain friendly changes to practice and to the library. Consider the following guiding questions. These will also be important to consider in revisiting the collection development plan.

- What is the philosophical underpinning of the school?
- What is the community like?
- How aware are the staff and leadership of brain and intelligence research?
- What about the student population? Describe the age group and any other factors of importance—for example, students may enroll at the school for an "arts" or "advanced science" program.
- Are there any other special programs offered in the school?
- What is offered both curricular and extracurricular?
- What is unique about the school?
- How would what is known about the brain and intelligence in learning via the current research impact or change the environment that the teacher-librarian works in every day?
- What will the interest level, acceptance, and assistance of the parents be like for brain friendly changes?
- How is the school library currently used?

BRAIN FRIENDLY SCHOOL LIBRARY GOALS

Once you have reflected on these areas, the teacher-librarian will want to develop or revise the school library goals to make them brain friendly, creating the practical steps on the way to achieving them. Two or three primary goals to work on over two or three years is usually manageable as the teacher-librarian begins implementation with introducing a variety of newer strategies. Goals and strategies need to be revisited annually—some years will require adjustment, and other years a great deal will be accomplished. Trying to accomplish too many goals too quickly can be unrealistic. Small steps, celebrated along the way, help to achieve the major goals over time.

The following three goals/achievement plans are what is suggested and expanded on in ensuing chapters of this book. These goals serve to create a larger framework that addresses the development of brain friendly school library practices.

GOAL 1:

Staff, students, and volunteers will work together to develop an *enriched environment* for a more brain friendly school library.

The achievement of this goal will involve the teacher-librarian focusing on staff development and engaging staff, students, and volunteers in making and implementing new decisions and practices around the school library's physical space, collection, policies, and learning styles.

GOAL 2:

The *intellectual climate* of the school library will become more brain friendly by focusing on a constructivist approach to research skills and processes.

The achievement of this goal will involve building an information literacy continuum for student learning involving relevance in project- and problem-based research activities.

GOAL 3:

Making more brain friendly *emotional connections* to literature, arts, and sciences will enhance memory and learning of cultural heritage.

The achievement of this goal will involve more sensory experiences, cooperative learning, and reflection/celebration.

BRAIN FRIENDLY SCHOOL LIBRARY POLICIES

Once goals, objectives, and strategies have been developed, teacher-librarians will want to closely examine the day-to-day operational policies of their school library and will be faced with rethinking some of them in more brain friendly ways as they address the first goal of creating an "enriched environment" for staff, students, and parents. Staff, students, and parents should already be familiar with current policies—hours of operation, how to book the library, materials sign-out procedures, overdues. It is a good idea to have policies printed and available in a staff handbook, online, or posted in the library and revisited annually. Teacher-librarians will initially want to discuss any changes in policies or common procedures with other school library staff, pages, and volunteers to determine how any proposed changes will affect their work with staff and students.

One "rule" or policy often practiced is "NO Food or Drink in the Library," as food or drink could be spilled on books or near technological devices. That is assuming that *all* students or staff are irresponsible. Knowing how important proper food and hydration are to the brain in the learning process, this could be approached much differently. In student and staff orientations to the school library, discuss the importance of proper food and nutrition to learning and encourage responsible use of water bottles or trips to the fountain. Discuss how to manage snacks in the library to preserve materials and safety issues with technology. Create compromise from "no food or drink" to responsible use, such as taking a "snack break" outside or having it a table without leaving a mess. Agree ahead of time as to logical consequences of not following through—cleaning it up, replacing materials, reduction of privileges, and so on. It is all about how learners want to be together in a neuron-enriching environment.

What about examining book exchange policies? Is it brain friendly to be only able to take out a book once a week on a class visit, whether the student needs to or not? Or are there other brain friendly ways to make sure students are developing in their reading practice and have access to the library? Teachers may have students keep reading logs and have systems set up so students know when it is appropriate to go to the library. When staff are not available for assistance for independent students accessing the library the full day, perhaps the first hour of the day—or whatever works at a particular school—would be available. Despite obstacles, with creative thinking, many solutions can be found for changing rules and policies that are not coherent with a brain friendly school library environment.

BRAIN FRIENDLY COLLECTION DEVELOPMENT

As the teacher librarian begins to plan and implement new or enhanced brain friendly school library learning experiences, the collection development plan will need to reflect needs that arise from this work with students and staff and support it. In a busy, active school library a rotating schedule for collection weeding and analysis is recommended, depending on the size of the collection and focusing on one section at a time. In a small elementary school, a teacher-librarian can usually attend to each section of the collection annually. In a larger high school, the rotation may occur over two or three years, depending on the teacher-librarian's schedule. Often, much can be accomplished in collection work during student exam weeks or prior to holiday breaks.

The written collection development plan should include an analysis of the rotation and collection; statement of responsibility, principles, criteria, and procedures for collection development; and a budget plan for acquiring new school library resources. In developing a brain friendly collection, standard collection development guidelines prevail—having resources that have been carefully evaluated by educators regarding authenticity, bias, currency, applicability, and durability for the students and the programs in the school. Quality resources emulate the healthy brain's intellectual, analytical way of operating. Remember that many key themes reflecting information literacy emerge repeatedly in brain research findings: The basic biological functions of the brain involve accessing, evaluating, and using information; creativity; story; lifelong continuous learning; collaboration. The collection must be current, appealing, and supportive of the needs of students and staff, with a good mix of classic works and current sources.

It is vitally important to use the teacher-librarian's expertise in collection development to teach and engage staff, students, and volunteers as applicable to the process so that they learn how to recognize authority and validity in resources in whatever format and understand the professional aspect of this part of the teacher-librarian's role. If a particular school library is in need of a major "weeding," the teacher-librarian might organize a "weed and feed" for the faculty by giving a brief overview of the collection development plan, explain how to tell if a resource is no longer useful to the school library, provide water and snacks, and ask teachers to work in their area of expertise. Two or three hours of this after school or on a professional day will accomplish a great deal, both in building collegiality and getting the job done.

Two of the first sections of the school library that would be recommended for weeding in a more brain friendly collection development approach would be the professional section and the biology/health sections. For the professional library, the school leadership team would be a valuable resource to assist with weeding and development. Although it is advisable for the staff to study a pertinent author or articles introducing brain research, they should be able to access additional resources or bibliographic recommendations from the school library. Sources in this book are recommended in chapter 1 and the References; additional sources/bibliographies abound on the Internet. Along with brain research resources, the professional library should also include resources relating to brain friendly educational methodology, such as materials both philosophical and practical relating to information literacy, cooperative learning, action research, intelligence, project-based learning, and so on.

BRAIN FRIENDLY STUDENT OUTCOMES

Reflecting on national or local information literacy standards and local curriculum outcomes and school programs, the teacher-librarian could develop cooperatively with teachers a list of learning outcomes that students need to achieve over time. Table 1 shows what that might look like for a brain friendly school library program focusing on an enriched environment, constructivist research, and emotional connections to literature and the arts. Many tenets of the outcomes can be introduced and/or reinforced across the grades as learner need dictates. Knowing the students, the teacher-librarian and teachers can best decide where they are in such a continuum.

Ideally, students would enter the continuum at kindergarten with basic steps into the outcomes on the chart through the collaborative school library program. They would exit high school with advanced abilities in information literacy. It would be a useful exercise for a teacher-librarian to look at the charts with the teachers and determine where the student profile is generally and what changes would be needed to be focused on for more brain friendly school library learning experiences. In addition, working with the teacher-librarians from feeder schools in sharing/developing the continuum would greatly enhance the movement of the student, K–12, through brain friendly information literacy skills and processes.

Table 1

An Enriched School Library Environment Will Enable Students to:

K 1 2 3 4 5 6 7 8 9 10 11 12

- Feel comfortable in communicating with the library staff for assistance, advice
- Feel safe and comfortable in the physical design of the library facility for multipurpose uses in their learning
- Feel part of making decisions around changes in their school library policies, space, or collection
- Understand why the environment is brain friendly and why that is important to how they learn and create memory
- Be responsible for care and return of materials in all formats and respectful in use of the library spaces
- Locate and select fiction, nonfiction, and media of interest to them using locations tools (Online Public Access Catalog [OPAC])

Engaging in Constructivist Research Students Will Be Able to:

K 1 2 3 4 5 6 7 8 9 10 11 12

- Develop a hypothesis from a research topic
- Share prior knowledge about the topic using a variety of graphic organizers
- Develop a series of focusing questions to develop the research

- Create a plan (goals) to conduct
  research on the topic with
  assistance from teacher/teacher-librarian
- Investigate resources in all
  formats to gain more knowledge
  on the topic (books, media,
  Web sites, journals), developing skills in:
  - how resources are organized
    (table of contents, index, search
    strategies, etc.)
  - note-taking (key words, phrases)
  - an understanding of currency/bias
  - recognizing/noting authority (bibliography)
- Determine and create
  other research tools to inform the hypothesis
  (interviews, surveys, experiments)
- Conduct the research plan
- Analyse patterns and themes
  informing hypothesis from research
  using a variety of analysis tools
  (colour coding, etc.)
- Make informed conclusions
- Present conclusion, choosing
  from a variety of presentation tools
  (PowerPoint, essay, poster,
  video, debate, mural, etc.)

Responding and Reflecting Emotionally to Literature and the Arts Students Will Be Able to:

- Appreciate and have access to
  a wide variety of
  authors, illustrators, artists
- Share prior knowledge about
  literature/arts
- Understand a variety of
  literary and artistic forms, genres
- Restructure, create, and communicate
  responses to literature and the arts
- Use a variety of oral formats to
  reflect on literature/arts
  (dialogue, discussion, debate)
- Use a variety of written formats to
  reflect on literature/arts (journals, poetry,
  diaries, etc.)
- Use a variety of dramatic formats to
  reflect on literature/arts (mime, improvisation,
  radio plays, readers' theatre, interviews,

K 1 2 3 4 5 6 7 8 9 10 11 12

dramatic monologue, scenes,
oral reading, videos, etc.)
- Use a variety of artistic formats to
  reflect on literature/arts (illustrator studies,
  dioramas, illustrated plot posters, paintings,
  picture books, sculpture, etc.)
- Use a variety of musical formats to
  reflect on literature/arts (writing songs,
  composing music using composing
  software, scores, or soundtracks, etc.)
- Use a variety of dance formats to
  reflect on literature/arts (choreograph a story
  plot, move as the character would, etc.)

Part II

GOAL 1: ENRICHED ENVIRONMENTS— TEACHER-LIBRARIAN AS STAFF DEVELOPER

Staff, students, and volunteers will work together to develop an enriched environment for a more brain friendly school library.

The achievement of this goal will involve the teacher-librarian focusing on staff development and engaging staff, students, and volunteers in making and implementing new decisions and practices around the school library's physical space, collection, policies, and learning styles.

Chapter 6

BRAIN FRIENDLY SPACE

In order to "set the stage" for constructivist research and emotional connection to literature and the arts, the physical space and operations for a more brain friendly school library will most likely need changing. Tight rows of shelves with few seating or working areas will not model the school library as a vital center of constructivist learning. Harshly enforced rules prohibiting unnecessary practices need to be reexamined to reduce threat and open the doors. The space must reflect the school's "learning laboratory," where innovative team teaching can be modeled and implemented by teacher-librarians in a practical, on-site daily manner as they team plan and teach with the faculty. Think of redesigning the space and how it operates as a cooperative adventure, like the many home design programs on television today! Engage the students, staff, and volunteers in a conversation around new ideas about how to design a comfortable brain friendly media center.

Think of this "learning laboratory" as a warm, inviting, welcoming place with stimulating work areas as well as reflective sites. Instead of a harsh, "hushed" environment, hear soft music, laughter, projects being worked on, students reading silently, orally, being read to, dialoguing. View multiple displays of student cognitive work such as poetry, art, sculpture, and Web pages that are altered every four to six weeks, as brains thrive on novelty. Have comfortable, functional furniture for working, reading, studying, and collaborating. Facilitate learning with warm, caring qualified personnel so that students feel supported, challenged, and trusted. When members of the learning community are partners with teacher-librarians in this endeavor, teacher-librarians will have their support and respect in operational policies and practices necessary to move forward with a brain friendly learning environment. In order to support a wide range of active learning in this "laboratory-type" setting, an example to share with staff, students, and volunteers might be the "Creative Learning Plaza," as detailed in chapter 1 (Creative Learning Systems 2004).

Similarly to television decorating shows, no matter what the school library budget turns out to be—along with help from students, staff, and community—the teacher-librarian can look closely at even the most challenging school library facility space and begin to create a brain-engaging environment based on rearranging what is there, scavenging school or district storage sites, and using "elbow grease" and paint and maybe even visiting a garage sale or two.

The teacher-librarian first will need to come up with a plan that suits the majority of the stakeholders in the re-creation of the library space. With staff and parents (volunteers), hold meetings, strike a committee/work group, or ask representatives to join a focus group to consider the redesign of the library space to make it more brain friendly. This can be a first comfortable step in introducing exciting concept changes that can occur via use of the school library facility with incorporation of and introduction to brain research and learning. With students, develop "student ambassadors" for the school library, similar to a student advisory group or school council team. This concept can be equally successful in elementary or secondary schools; kindergarten ambassadors have done as well in presenting ideas and working in the library as the older students. All students need to feel welcomed (or mentored, if necessary) in such a group.

To develop a team of student library ambassadors, a number of ways could be employed, depending on the nature of the school. Depending on the size of the school, it is important to have one or two ambassadors from each class or division in a larger setting. Decide if this group's function will be to help with the redesign of the library space or if this group will continue to meet and work on other aspects of the brain friendly school library on an ongoing or annual basis. Homeroom teachers could nominate individuals for school library ambassadors, request two volunteers, or hold elections if there is greater interest. Perhaps in larger secondary schools these could be positions on the student council. Reflect on the student population and decide what would work best to get students involved.

School library ambassadors can then go back to the classrooms and ask classmates about ideas for changes in the school library or hold contests for design drawings. A key concept in brain research is student decision making and democratic learning; the teacher-librarian or teachers need to explain to the students that although not all of the ideas coming in may be practical or implemented, they will be considered as part of the overall committee work in making the school library more brain friendly. Depending on the ages or readiness of the students, they could volunteer or take turns presenting their ideas to the staff/volunteer committee.

Committee, ambassador, or volunteer meetings—and/or a combination of such groups—should be designed using brain friendly principles as a way to begin to model newer learning paradigms. It is a good idea to provide prereading to members with a short article or recommended Web site about current brain research principles and educational practice so that participants who wish to come to the session with background can do so. Provide water glasses or bottles and a nutritious snack or two (pretzels, carrot sticks) and explain why these items are being provided. Start with a warm-up activity, such as a "true/false" quiz that includes statements such as "We have only been able to study the living brain for about the past five years" or "A brain friendly school library will always be noisy" or "Brain research will affirm/change my practice." Following is as an example of a brain friendly session outline that could be adapted for use with staff, student ambassadors, and parent volunteers.

Introducing Brain Research

- Goal: To redesign the school library to make it more "brain friendly."
- Watch the video *Bringing Brain Research into Classroom Practice: Program 3: An Enriched Environment for Learning* (*Video Journal of Education* 1997).
- After viewing, request participants to take a few moments to list their perceptions of a "rich learning environment."
- Ask participants to join with two others and share their perceptions.
- Using larger chart paper and coloured pencils or felt pens, have the smaller groups draw/map out what they imagine a brain friendly school library would look like.
- Post and share the drawings, noting similarities. Use these at the next meeting to brainstorm a list of potential changes to prioritize.
- Provide homework: Select an article or Web site on enriched environments for preparation for the next meeting.

It will be important to point out to the students, committees, or focus groups that the redesign should incorporate areas for multifunctional learning activities—cognitive space—and storing of resources in a realistic light, given the size of your school library and budget. The underlying concept of brain friendly learning focuses on the concept of active learning, defined as "most students active most of the time." This can be viewed in two aspects. One aspect involves exploration and inquiry, emotional expressions of interaction with literature and the arts, dialogue, debate, cooperative learning, team teaching, and information literacy experiences. Space in the redesign must consider these perhaps more unfamiliar functions in the school library. This may be a change from an environment where patrons are used to being told to be "quiet" or to sit individually to study. The other aspect of active learning can be thought of as the more introspective—meaning that space also needs to be provided for quieter reflective or studious activities such as reading, note-taking, journaling, individual work on computers, even sketching or painting at times.

Consider the following guiding questions pertaining to the two aspects of active learning in the brain friendly school library for school libraries from kindergarten through high school. For those questions that are desirable and cannot be accommodated through inexpensive or creative means, consider building those into a brain friendly school library budget plan for future consideration, fund-raising, or grant-writing projects.

I. Facility space for team teaching, cooperative learning, dialogue, presentation:

- Depending on the size of the school, are there one to three areas of table groupings that could accommodate a class (classes) working in the library? Ordering over thirty new library chairs at $100 each to seat a class versus discovering thirty used ones from another school in the school district and having them recovered at $10 a chair or steam cleaned can leave much more money for resources.

- Are there stations or groupings of computers available for teaching or project work and use of the Internet?

- If a computer lab of some sort is not available in the library, are wireless laptops available or worth investing in to create groupings of computers for multiple purposes without having to consider more furnishing?

- Is there an area(s) where students can access and use digital cameras? Video cameras? Scanners or other peripherals such as a "SMART Board" (an electronic screen that can be connected to a computer)?

- Is there an area where students can record voice, music?

- Is there a "story corner" (elementary) or open area (amphitheatre) where storytelling, movement, and drama can occur?

II. Facility space for reading, studying, individual project work:

- Can bookshelves be lined up against walls or put into a series of "pods" to create open working spaces?

- Can bookshelves frame more reflective spaces?

- Can fiction shelving or racks back or frame a reading area with comfortable chairs, coffee tables, area rugs, plants, a fish tank, a ready display of new materials?

- If short on space, can reading "corners" be established with side tables or baskets displaying new or favourite resources, periodicals?

- Can shelving display examples of sculpture, models, dioramas—especially those created by the students?

- Are books and other materials on the shelves displayed pleasingly, with room on the shelves to display new or interesting items?

- Was the library constructed with standard "library carrels"? Can they accommodate individual study, listening to compact discs (CDs)? Could art students or volunteers, to make them more appealing, paint them? Could shelf ends also be painted with art?

- Paint the entranceway to the library or otherwise make it as welcoming as possible.

- Is there room/equipment for an individual video or DVD (digital video disc) viewing station?

- Are computer stations, stand-alone or laptop, available for individual use?

To further stimulate the brain, reduce threat, and provide comfortable learning, space aesthetics also need to be considered. The brain friendly school library should be safe, clean, and spacious. For example, once furniture, shelves, technology, and resources had been relocated or rearranged, the committee might end up dusting, whitewashing the walls, and renting a carpet/upholstery cleaner. Many new school libraries are being built with tile flooring instead of carpet, as in the past, particularly in tabled areas. Recycling and trash bins need to be handy.

Arranging to play soft music in the background makes the environment more pleasant for students and staff. This is a good opportunity to showcase new or classical CDs from the library collection or play a radio station that is known for classical or soothing music. Student ambassadors or pages can help to take care of plants or fish added to beautify the environment as part of their duties. Initially, they could research what type of plant or animal life would do well in an indoor environment, based on access to light and other factors.

Whitewashed walls make a great space for displaying a regular rotation of framed student art work, another duty that library pages, art students, or volunteers can take on. If the school library has bulletin boards in the facility, paint them a soothing colour such as light blue and aesthetically display student library projects, posters, or larger paintings. There are many resources available on the aesthetics of display including involving the opinion of a local artist. Have a well-organized, up-to-date bulletin board for posting information, events, ideas, and school library news.

Operational policies in the school library may have become routine with the school library staff. Opening these for discussion with the committee and stakeholder groups around brain friendly practices will give the teacher-librarian feedback for responding to and addressing merited changes. Questions to consider here include:

- How will access to the brain friendly facility be provided?
- Will students have free access at all hours? What are the library opening hours that current staff can provide?
- How can independent users feel comfortable in getting assistance from school library staff?
- What procedures must the students and staff know for checking out resources—amounts, time, responsibility around?
- Will staff and students need orientations around using the online catalogue?
- What procedures must the students and staff know for use of any of the spaces or technologies set up in the library?
- Will there be Internet access after hours?
- How can a class book the facility? The teacher-librarian? Areas of the library?
- Will all classes have annual or regular orientations to the library to discuss use and policies?
- What will be seen as respectful around student conduct, noise level, and food and drink in the facility?

As the committee or work group thinks about these questions, others will come to mind in changes or new ideas needed to make the school library space and policies more brain friendly. Collectively, students, staff, and volunteers committed to this first and basic series of changes with enriching the school library's physical space and operational policies will be ready to move on to consider more brain friendly changes to other aspects of the school library and its programs, where an enriched environment also means one that is intellectually enriching.

Following are three cooperatively planned library projects at different grade levels (primary, middle school, high school) that can contribute to the enriched environment.

PRIMARY

The following two activities can occur simultaneously by dividing the class in two and then rotating the groups.

"Dewey Art"

- Have students choose a favourite nonfiction topic.
- Have them (or assist them) in printing the topic on a large recipe-type card. For example, "Bears," "Dinosaurs," or "Trucks."
- Take them to the bookshelves and point out where books on their favourite topic are found. Have each student select a book on his or her topic.
- Upon returning to the cards, have them write the Dewey number of their topic next to the printed word on the card: "Bears—550."
- Have them illustrate the topic using pencil, crayons or watercolour pencils. "Frame" their artwork with construction paper, having them do borders and so on. Rotate displays of their artwork near the Dewey section they illustrate.

"Plastecine Alphabet"

- Remind students that fiction books are arranged by author's last name alphabetically.
- Assign each student a letter of the alphabet. Have them create the letter using colourful plastecine on heavier card paper, 8×11 inches. Have them create a symbol for the letter—apple for A, and so on.
- Rotate displaying the letters by the "A" books, "B" books, and so on.

MIDDLE SCHOOL

"Dewey Paintings"

- Have students in groups assigned to each section of the library.
- Let them explore the sections, seeing what kinds of books reside in the 100s, 500s, 800s, and so forth.

- Using the books as inspiration, have them create watercolour paintings (8×11 inches) that symbolize the theme of that Dewey section. Invest in inexpensive frames to frame and mount their paintings near the sections, rotating them if there are a large number of students.

- If watercolour is not possible, any other form of representation works, from pencil crayon drawings to magazine collage. (Have students cut out and collage an 8×11 inch representation of a Dewey section from magazine discards.)

HIGH SCHOOL

"Art Project"

- Taken a step further in high school, work with the art department in creating a variety of visual representations of sections of the library.

- Have art students assigned to a section and work with the teacher-librarian and the teacher to decide how they will create a work of art to represent a section of the library.

- Hopefully, students will find a number of ways to represent the library holdings—a sculpture symbolizing the sciences? A painting of William Shakespeare? A digital travelogue of the geography section continually playing on a DVD?

Chapter 7

RESOURCE-BASED LEARNING— COLLECTION

> Resource-based learning is a philosophy based on beliefs of how children learn best, practiced by many teachers and in the works of many theorists from John Dewey to those now exploring the potential of the Internet.
>
> *(Brown 1997)*

A brain friendly school library with bright, open, inviting spaces requires the collection, that multiplicity of learning resources, to also reflect brain friendly challenges and to be current, weeded, aesthetically displayed, and accessible both physically and intellectually to the student population. The brain needs opportunities to select the best information from a wide variety of resources, both human and multimedia. This provides increased input and variety to the brain, growing those dendrites and neural connections. "Resource-based learning," a term coined earlier in school library literature, denotes this special relationship that exists between using a wide variety of resources in multiple formats to support curriculum and school programs, rather than relying primarily on lecture and textbook. By learning from a vast array of resources, the learner takes steps in the growth of becoming information literate.

To this day, many school library collections are largely print dependent. But this does not have to reflect negatively. The twenty-first-century publishing industry thrives alongside the Internet and other forms of media. The last decade has seen the explosion of both the supersized bookstore (Chapters, Indigo, Borders, Barnes and Noble) independents and the supersized media outlets. School libraries have the challenge of balancing a school collection with the continual outpouring of new resources and deciding which items to maintain as "brain friendly" sources. "Books" often receive poor press owing to the fact that many libraries keep dusty or even poorly written volumes that have passed their time or suffered from neglect—again, in both physical and intellectual senses.

Consumers at Chapters or other similar venues are free to purchase whatever catches their eye or whimsy. If it turns up at a garage sale later, so be it. But libraries are founded on principles of careful selection and collection analysis. Libraries for schools are entrusted with this task of selecting the very best resources to capture the intellect and imagination of the students and are often challenged to do this on very tight budgets. And publishing, like anything else, goes through waves and trends, leaving many books purchased and unread on school library shelves that may have been added in original school start-up collections or mass-purchasing efforts. Compare this to a clothing wardrobe: There are classic items used or replaced or updated year after year and trendy or flawed items the owner wished he or she had never purchased. Some individuals pack these errors off to charity or other places, and others cannot find the good items with all the extraneous items jammed around them. When developing school library collections, the teacher-librarian should not do anything but strive for the best—indeed, the best of the best—for the student's learning needs.

Students from kindergarten through high school need to be able to access excellent learning resources, both modern and classical. A better term perhaps is "finely written or composed material," and it is the content in resources that is critically important to being brain friendly. It holds in many cases that the format most adults or children still enjoy for a good read or in-depth look at a subject is a printed book. Imbedded here are the stories of our culture and other cultures and characters and plots that feed the collective psyche. Within finely written nonfiction print, information is found that has been carefully and authoritatively researched over time, information that can be used to compare to the instant information constantly bombarding us from newspapers, television, the Internet. As Ellen Langer reminded us in chapter 2 of this book, what was once fiction can become fact, and vice versa.

What makes a brain friendly resource? A brain friendly resource is going to be one that meets standards, long held and devised, of resource evaluation. This is where teacher-librarian education is vital to the evaluation of learning resources and, more important, to teaching others to evaluate resources so that teachers, students, and parents begin to ask pertinent questions regarding resources. How many of them read reviews for plays, movies, or books in the weekend newspaper? If they do, can they concur with or blatantly disagree with a reviewer? Do they have the tools to evaluate and make an informed judgment to support their opinions?

The common standards for resource evaluation are listed below. Any resource should reflect the intellectual range of students and be informative without being condescending or too narrow in focus. There is a lot of "junk" out there, and a human life span is finite; students need to learn tools to guide them to resources that will be worthy of their time and intellect. Primarily, resources of all formats should be:

- Current
- Relevant
- Accurate
- Aesthetically pleasing
- Accessible
- Durable

The best way to judge a resource, of course, is to read it, view it, listen to it, experience it, compare or contrast it with similar materials and then ultimately to discuss it with others. It is also wise and can be time saving to research reviews. This is entirely possible to expect when teaching evaluative tools to a class studying a certain group of authors or a controversial subject. For teachers who say they do not have time for this close look at resources and media with students, they must look closely at the state or provincial curriculum. Most of them in this day and age have moved from topical, fact-based to process-oriented, critical thinking skills. Gone should be the days when a resource is used primarily to deliver content—the "content deliverer" needs to be assessed for accuracy, bias, and all the other attributes of the evaluative process. Time spent here and not on a lot of busy work will serve to prepare the students for their future as independent information literate citizens.

It is largely impractical at times for the teacher-librarian to be able to analyse all the resources in the collection when dealing with a full school library collection. If the teacher-librarian is new to a school, it will take him or her awhile to learn the collection. This collection has been built up over time likely based on a starter collection put in place when the school was first opened. During times when the brain friendly library is not humming with activity, the teacher-librarian needs to set aside time for applying brain friendly principles to collection development and eventually dealing with each and every resource item, new and old. Using brain friendly principles, ask:

- Does this resource (book, film, Web site, print, software program, periodical) contain an "enriched cognitive environment"—current, relevant, accurate, aesthetically pleasing, accessible, durable?
- What is its relevance quotient—will the student or user be challenged, delighted, nonthreatened, taken to a new place of discovery with this resource?
- Will the student then be able to construct new knowledge based on having interacted with the resource?
- Does the resource lend itself to interdisciplinary connections?
- Does the resource lead one to think and reflect?
- Does the resource evoke a sensory response, whether joyful or sad, and lead the user away from sameness or mediocrity?

When teacher-librarians start examining items in a collection in this light, they will find themselves getting increasingly selective in what they add to it or purchase. Teacher-librarians' own biological brains will respond to the resource as students' or other readers' will—a quality resource will delight them, surprise them, and take them to new places. Teacher-librarians will want to rely less on reviews and more on their own evaluative skills or the teachers' and students' as teacher-librarians involve them in collection analysis. Past time-saving methods will not pay off; the shelves may not be jammed as before, but the shelves will have more brain friendly items. The teacher librarian will also rely less on the "tried and true," one tenet of collection purchase where trust is given that a noted author, often with passable reviews, would be a fine addition without a firsthand look at the resource. Many seasoned authors seemed to be turning out seasonal books for the sake of a commercial or religious holiday, yet this alone does not make them seasonal or religious classics. Teacher-librarians must take the time to examine purchases they are considering for a brain friendly collection. This helps budgets as well, as fewer items may be purchased, but the students will be getting greater quality in what is purchased.

This is easier with picture books, prints, periodicals, and Web sites. With novels, nonfiction tomes, and films, especially in secondary schools, the task of determining "cognitive excellence" in resources is much more time-consuming owing to the depth and length of the content. Here reviews beckon, colleagues are relied on, and student opinion contributes. Still, teacher-librarians are advised to at least view the item and attempt to read a few pages or view a segment to get an idea of the flavour of the item, to determine if a student interacting with it will be enriched.

Another tool for engaging others in collection development revolves around designing cooperative units based on evaluation. Although the humanities (language arts and social studies) are ideally suited to these units, any subject works and should be considered—the sciences, arts, mathematics. Following is a sampling of six such ideas suggested for various grade levels. Depending on a school's level of library or technology use, the ideas could be adapted for any or all of the levels.

PRIMARY

"Picture Book Talks"

- The teacher-librarian selects a number of classic and new picture books with the primary teacher(s) he or she is working with. Display them on tables or in the "story corner" of the library.
- Have the class gather around the books. Point out to the students that they will be doing a book talk so that everyone will learn about many more titles to read. Choose a favourite book and demonstrate sharing it with the students through a simple book talk.
- Include the concepts of evaluation in the demonstration: Is the book new? Old? How can you tell? If it is old, is it still important today? If it is new, is it meaningful today? Is it pleasing to look at? Talk about the art in the illustrations. Is the story clear and interesting? Share information about the author. What is liked (or not liked) about the book?
- Indicate that the student's future book talk should include the title, author, and theme or main idea that the book is about. It should include statements of evaluation as stated in the questions above. Have them include a brief, prepared reading from part of the book, without giving away the ending. The teacher-librarian may find that some students will

review a book negatively, and students should know and understand that that is okay if they have followed the process of review accurately.

- Have the students select a book to read for their own book talk. Some students may need to try a few books prior to selecting the one that they will share. Rehearse with students as they prepare for their book talk. Some students may wish to memorize their talk; others could use "recipe" cards to record their notes.

- Once a week, have "book talk day" where a student (or a few students) shares his or her book talk with the class in the library. Make it special by inviting parents or other special guests (the principal, resource teacher, etc.) to attend if possible.

"I'm the Expert!"

- Select a number of new and standard primary nonfiction books on a number of different subjects that the teacher-librarian or teachers have noted as "hot topics" among the students (e.g., pet books, car and trucks, beginning science books). Display them on tables in the library.

- Point out to the students that they will be sharing a book talk with the class on one of their favourite nonfiction subjects. They will be able to learn more about their favourite subject and present the reading behind it.

- Choose a favourite subject and demonstrate sharing it with the students. Include the concepts of evaluation more pertinent to nonfiction in the demonstration: Is the book new? Old? How can you tell? If it is old, is it still important information? How can you tell? Is it pleasing to look at? Talk about the art in the illustrations. Does the art support or detract from learning about the subject? Is the writing interesting and understandable? What is liked (or not liked) about the book? What is learned about the subject?

- Indicate that their talk should include the title, author, and subject that the book is about. It should include statements of evaluation as stated in the questions above. Have them point out a page of the book that includes a favourite new fact on the subject. The teacher-librarian may find that some students will negatively review a book, and they should know and understand that that is okay if they have followed the process of review accurately.

- Have the students select a book to read for their own subject book talk. Some students may wish to have assistance selecting a book about a subject that was not pulled for the initial display. Rehearse with students as they prepare for their book talk. Again, some students may wish to memorize their talk; others could use "recipe" cards to record their notes. Students could be encouraged to bring or make something that represents the subject—their pet hamster, a rock collection, for example.

- This time, schedule an "expert"-sharing sharing week and have four or five experts share per day with the class in the library. Invite parents or other special guests to attend if possible.

MIDDLE SCHOOL

"Book Net with Artistic Representation"

- The teacher-librarian selects a number of classic and new novels with the language arts teacher(s) he or she is working with. Display the books on tables in the library.

- Choose a favourite and demonstrate sharing it with the students through a simple book talk that includes the elements of evaluation—currency, relevance, accuracy, aesthetics, accessibility, and durability.

- Point out to the students that they will be doing a book review for the school library's Web site so that many more students can learn about many more titles. Their write-up should include the title, author, and theme or main idea that the book is about. It should include statements of evaluation—relevance, aesthetics, and engagement. Remind them that all reviews may not be positive.

- The students will also be required to create an artistic representation of the book. This can be in any form they choose—a painting, model, diorama, and so on. It can be added to the written work on the Web site using a scanner or digital camera.

- Set due dates for the project and have the students learn to put it on the Web site along with their representation. If desired, an internal "chat room" can be created among the classes to debate the reviews.

"Take Five!"

- This project in evaluation involves the teacher-librarian working with the social studies teacher(s) in a curricular area related to studying another country.

- Using India as an example, display materials (including fiction) from the collection on the topic around five or six different tables. Items may be borrowed in addition from other libraries or loan pools if possible.

- The teacher-librarian and teacher will provide each student with a statement that will lead to knowledge needed in the study. For example: "The primary religion in India is——" "Most people in India today do not believe in a caste system——" "The major export in India is——"

- Have the students use at least five resources from their table to prove or dispel the "fact." Have them create a poster with the fact on the top and a quote about the fact from each source. End the poster with a statement of opinion from the student based on what he or she has discovered. Post the posters in the library.

HIGH SCHOOL

"Book TV"

- The teacher-librarian and English teacher(s) select a number of new novels or nonfiction books that merit better circulation among the students. Display them on tables in the library.

- Choose a favourite and demonstrate sharing it with the students by the teacher-librarian and teacher doing a mock interview as if reviewing the book on a television talk show. Include the elements of evaluation—currency, relevance, accuracy, aesthetics, accessibility, and durability.

- Point out to the students that they will be doing a book review with a partner for the school library's "television station" so that students can learn about many more titles. Their interview should include the title, author, and theme or main idea that the book is about. It should include statements of evaluation—relevance, aesthetics, and engagement. Remind them that all reviews may not be positive. Each partner will alternate the role of reviewer/interviewer.

- A schedule for videotaping will need to be created. Encourage the students to be creative with their "book show" personas.

- Depending on the level of technology available at the school, the interviews could be shared within a class as a videotape, on the Web site, or playing in the library on a continuous video or resource for finding out about new books.

"Proving My Point!"

- Working with the science and humanities teacher(s), the teacher-librarian and teachers put together a "mock trial" project based on a piece of literature that deals with a controversial science topic, such as the play *Twelve Angry Men* (Darwinism) or any other topic where two opposing viewpoints can be researched and presented through both literature and scientific resources.

- Organize the class into debate teams and have students examine a number of resources that represent both sides of the issue, current and historical, "fictional" and factual.

- Use standard debate practices and rules: Students will, and should, form their own opinions on the issue but must be prepared to present their assigned side of the debate.

- In creating arguments to engage in a debate about the issue, have students also include an evaluation of the resources using the elements of evaluation—source, currency, relevance, accuracy, aesthetics, accessibility, and durability.

- Arrange to host the mock trial(s) in the library—inviting special guests and/or videotaping the event.

Chapter 8

LEARNING STYLES—MEMORY

Once a school community has started to redesign the school library physical space and collection, it is time to go deeper and delve into changing or enhancing teaching practice within the library to reflect brain research and recommended pedagogical shifts. A good entry point is to examine the concept of memory, as all teachers, including the teacher-librarian, hope that what they are teaching will be learned, remembered, and practiced by students!

Many teachers find themselves on the "standards driven, achievement test" racetrack, trying to cover curriculum at lightning speed, pouring facts into students, hoping they will remember. Most students—indeed, many teachers—have never been taught about memory and the best ways to actually "memorize"—from preparing for standard tests, rote basics, or on to complex, higher-order thinking and performance tasks. Educators need to facilitate this process in a spirit of inclusion where learning disabilities are seen as learning differences as individuals bring varying cultures, learning styles, personality styles, intelligences, and energy levels to the learning process.

Many teachers who see or believe in the benefit of working with a teacher-librarian in collaborative planning, teaching, research, and other aspects of the school library program may not take the next step to actually planning units with the teacher-librarian, owing to their "coverage" driven, time-consuming practices. For teacher-librarians to take the leadership in introducing brain friendly practices is an important step in establishing their role in learning leadership, collaborative planning and teaching, and staff development so that the importance of connecting the school library program to co-achieving curricular goals can be actualized. Teachers may think they do not have the time for library projects or research, but if they are working with the teacher-librarian around neuroscience-based practices that will also help them in their daily work, they are more likely to try something "new."

Memory is often broadly described as being of two primary types—a spatial memory system (long term) and a set of systems for rote learning (short term). The brain understands and remembers best when facts and skills are embedded in natural spatial or long-term memory. Following the work of Marilyn Sprenger (1999), brain research points to many additional memory routes that, when focused on for a specific purpose, lead to deeper learning and understanding. The teacher-librarian and teacher could strategically plan activities to coincide with five related memory factors, as discussed in chapter 1 of this book:

1. Semantic (word memory of an event/learning experience)
2. Emotional (feelings at the time of event/learning)
3. Automatic (conditioned response memory to event/learning)
4. Episodic (location-oriented memory of the event/learning)
5. Procedural (movements occurring during the event/learning).

The following columns illustrate how this might look in three levels of school library research projects using the common science topic example of "Plants," remembering that in the learning process the various memory types overlap, intersect, and support each other.

Primary: How Our Garden Grows

Memory Focus	Library Strategy
Semantic	Graphic organizer: simple Web pre-research to brainstorm current knowledge of the subject "Where does our food come from?"
Automatic	Mini-lessons on food facts
	Create charts around the room for where various foods originate
Episodic	Students relate stories of buying/growing food to share with class
Emotional	Guest speaker from local food bank gives presentation; students paint to music feelings after the presentation
Procedural	Students plant a "food bank" garden after researching what food plants grow best in their geographic area (e.g., potatoes, carrots, zucchini)

Middle School: Local Trees/Forests

Memory Focus	Library Strategy
Semantic	Graphic organizer: simple Web pre-research to brainstorm current knowledge of the subject "Can you name indigenous species of trees?"
Automatic	Mini-lessons on local tree/forest facts
	Create diagrams/charts of information

Episodic	Students journal about a time they were visiting a local nature trail or enjoying trees in their yards or neighbourhood
Emotional	Students research into local issues involving forest ecology, for example, logging, urbanization, and write an emotional response to what they discover
Procedural	Students decide on an action to make an impact on the issue, for example, writing letters to Congress or the city, creating posters of awareness, writing and putting on a play for the community around the issue

High School: Rainforest Ecology

Memory Focus	Library Strategy
Semantic	Graphic organizer: simple Web pre-research to brainstorm current knowledge of the subject "Rainforest Ecology—Global Support or Disaster?"
Automatic	Mini-lessons on rainforest issues
	Note-taking strategies reinforced using PMI (plus/minus/interesting fact) charting
Episodic	Students in pairs, small groups, then whole class dialogue about when and if they have personally or the community has been personally affected regarding rainforest issues (e.g., product consumption, construction)
Emotional	Have students bring selections of current music that relate to their feelings on rainforest destruction
	Selections can be played as students are encouraged to write poetry based on their feelings
Procedural	Have students in groups prepare debates relating to rainforest issues
	Develop clear rubrics around the debate
	Vote on the strongest debate team based on the rubrics
	Have this team share the debate at a school assembly, local news channel, school Web site, or other event

As the sample planning ideas illustrate, planning for instruction varies depending on what serves the memory best for long-term learning. Increasingly, the sample strategies mirror what successful twenty-first-century work places are demanding—the ability to build on knowledge, collaborate, compare, contrast, debate, create, activate.

The following workshop suggested below offers a way for the teacher-librarian to introduce teachers to brain friendly practices that impact all memory types. The steps of the workshop can be done in a variety of ways depending on the size of the faculty or the structure of the school's meeting or professional development times. This process can occur in a series of after school sessions, a half-day session, or a couple of two-hour sessions. Ideally, if the school is delving into brain friendly practices in a bigger way each professional day of the school year would focus on the brain, including ongoing book studies, planning, and sharing of experiences. Patterning this book, the initial focus would rest on studying and creating enriched environments, followed by enriched constructivist practice, then working toward more "emotional" environments. If it is a safer step to start smaller at a school, the entire process can focus on just moving toward a more brain friendly library space, and over time with the school library's central role in the school, changes will inspire and permeate growth in practice. It is again recommended that the teacher-librarian hold a post on the school professional development committee or aspire to chair or co-chair this group in the role as learning leader.

Workshop 2: Introducing Teachers to Brain Compatible Practice

- Provide a couple of short readings for teachers to preread prior to the workshop.
- Provide nutritious snacks, water bottles, and a brain friendly opening activity, such as a "true/false" sheet with brain research facts.
- Show additional videos that focus directly on brain friendly pedagogical practices or take time to go through one of the Web sites relating to brain research and learning and discuss these along with the preread article.
- Have teachers dialogue about the information presented. Depending on the size of the group, have different groups dialogue about different questions and record their thoughts on chart paper. Share through using cooperative learning techniques such as the "fishbowl" where one volunteer from each group comes to the centre of the groups and summarises their talk. Sample dialogue questions could be:
  - How can a focus on curriculum coverage be detrimental to comprehension and long-term memory? What practices could relate to long-term memory retention? How can school library learning experiences be collaboratively developed along these lines?
  - What is the difference between thematic topics like "change" versus "dinosaurs"? How can the school library become involved in integrated thematic planning?
- And/or provide chart paper, felts. Have teachers draw/design a brain-based school incorporating the school library.
- And/or have teachers in groups of four with large chart paper. Each teacher should have a different coloured felt pen so that the four colours reflect the coming together of four ideas. Assign the problem: How would you plan and teach a unit on_____based on brain research incorporating the school library? Share by having one person stay in the group; the others rotate to view the other charts or add ideas. Post in the library— implement!
- Follow-up: The teacher-librarian arranges to meet with grade teachers or teams to collaborate on a brain friendly school library project.

An ultimate goal of educators is to develop brain friendly practices that ensure learning is meaningful, applicable, and life enhancing. In this it is hoped that processes are provided that strengthen long- and short-term memory functions so that learners do not "forget" useless dogma often fed to them at school upon entry to the "real" world. In the next two parts of this book, various educational methodologies that are brain friendly will be explored—some quite familiar to school libraries and others that may not be. These methods are related in separate chapters to permit a closer examination of them and ideas around their implementation in a brain friendly school library learning experience. However, aspects of each method naturally or strategically occur or overlap. Cooperative learning is discussed through setting up cooperative learning library centers, yet cooperative learning lends itself to the very essence of project work, sensory work, and other information literacy learning experiences. Inquiry or action research can formulate the foundation for project work, and so on. Ultimately, moving into brain friendly methodology in collaborative school library experiences will propel the school library into an active, dynamic "learning central" core of the school.

Part III

GOAL 2: INTELLECTUAL ENVIRONMENTS— TEACHER-LIBRARIAN AS INFORMATION LITERACY AGENT

The intellectual climate of the school library will become more brain friendly by focusing on a constructivist approach to research skills and processes.

The achievement of this goal will involve building an information literacy continuum for student learning involving relevance in project and problem based research activities.

Chapter 9

INQUIRY AND ACTION RESEARCH

Traditionally, one of the key uses for school or other library settings has been research papers or projects. Many large university, college, and public libraries have staff librarians assigned as research librarians. Research ranges from the user wanting a simple answer to a question to those working on doctoral dissertations. In the school library, students seek information on questions and subjects they are curious about, as well as working on larger-scale projects and papers. In the dusty domains of libraries past, information was often difficult to access or unavailable. Early goals of teacher-librarians were to move students toward becoming increasingly independent in being able to access and use information. Many research projects emulated traditional classroom practices of gathering and repeating rote facts, such as using a book or encyclopaedia to "find out" about an animal's food, habitat, and appearance. Or to look up an article on "World War II" and answer a list of questions provided by the teacher.

Today, we live in the world of "information overload." It is everywhere and every place, easily available in every form and point of view. Increasingly, researchers, especially students in school, turn to the Internet for information. The role of the teacher-librarian has taken a quantum leap, becoming associated with the term "information literacy" and generating a great deal of research and exemplary practice around developing tomorrow's citizens into independent, responsible—indeed ethical—lifelong learners, users, and *creators* of information. It is incomprehensible that in this age of burgeoning information and communication technologies, this global frontier, that most provinces in Canada and some areas of the United States are bereft of teacher-librarians. How can this be intellectually good for the developing brains of students?

Brain research points to the brain's innate purpose of searching for meaning through patterns or patterning. The functioning brain actually patterns the processes of inquiry and action research. It questions, with questions encouraging neural branching. According to information/ technology expert Jamie Mackenzie (1997), "[Q]uestions are our primary technological tool, they are what makes us human." From questions, the brain seeks patterns: What context is the inquiry set in? What do I hypothesize the answer(s) to be? What is the issue for me? What information is already known about it? What are my goals, outcomes, and plans around the questions? The quest? What do I need to do? What interventions and plans are possible and productive? What patterns am I seeing emerge from my data? What major themes? Conclusions? New questions? The brain is biologically netted and comfortable with this process. Is this how inquiry and research look in school's today? As we move toward constructivist learning and teaching systems, the roles of student and teacher or teacher-librarian and concepts of knowledge shift as demonstrated in Table 2.

Many teachers today do embrace a more constructivist approach to learning. Often, they will be the teachers most comfortable in partnering with a teacher-librarian to develop authentic research experiences involving the school library. Others remain in the classroom, or computer lab, questioning the impact of the school library around traditional or twenty-first-century research practices. Most still defend the library's literature collection but raise the question, "Who needs books any more for research?"

Table 2

Concept of Knowledge: Curriculum:	Instruction:	Learning:	
	Teacher/Teacher- Librarian Roles	*Learner Roles*	
Transformation Theory	*Guide*	*Frustration*	Inquiry
Content-Learner	*Mentor*	*Error*	Generative
Constructs	*Facilitator*	*Explorer*	Clear Object
Developmental	*Critical Friend*	*Discoverer*	Resource-Based
Systems	*Work with*	*Active*	Projects
Problems	*Open Questions*	*Reason*	Interdisciplinary
Knowledge within Learner	*Collaborative*	*Engaged*	Comparative
"Seeing" the Learner	*Researcher*	*Whole*	
Constructivist	*Teams*	*Self-Reliant*	Wisdom
		Cooperative	Connected
		Ownership	Self-Monitoring
		Application	
		Lifelong	
		Reflective	
		Infer	
		Predict	

Source: Sykes 2002, 42.

Books (and other resource formats) of course are invaluable if a school library collection is brain friendly—current, weeded, and contains information in a wide variety of formats. Whether on the shelf or online, teachers and students should be comfortable with and aware that school library resources support their construction of knowledge in the realm of intellectual freedom. Here is a place where views are presented objectively, "one of our last democratic institutions." Here is a place where students from kindergarten to graduation can learn not only how to access information but how to evaluate it to develop curious, questioning, thinking brains. Here is a place where current books and reference sources can be used to validate information heard on television or found on the Internet, and topics can become bigger themes using authentic research as a way to search for meaning. Here the domains of knowledge can interconnect; "science" and "social studies" and "literature" are not separate subjects in coming to terms with deep meaning around relevant issues.

School libraries are natural sources of complexity in learning where domains of knowledge, between and beyond "subjects," can be connected. The major domains of knowledge encompass the sciences, technology, humanities, and the arts and are translated into various courses or subjects or curriculums—language arts, English, math, algebra, biology, and so on. The teacher-librarian can study and use the interdisciplinary approach to further collaborative teamwork and student achievement by working with two or more teachers from a variety of departments—for example, the history, English, and drama teachers prepare an integrated inquiry project around a history topic. Or, in a smaller setting, plan with an elementary teacher to incorporate learning from science, literature, and music together for an inquiry project. The "discipline" is the means to an end; inquiry must involve the student in the processes of authentic, meaningful, relevant research. The "pasts" and "presents" inherent within the domains of knowledge must make room to connect to the student's world and future.

To visit and revisit questions with disciplinary knowledge, inquiry, and interdisciplinary vehicles, longer periods of time or better uses of time are critical. Involving multiple subject goals/teachers is one strategy. Developing a long-range timetable for the school library to include every class or student in a brain friendly inquiry project, at least once or twice a year, depending on the size of the school, is another. The teacher-librarian could post such a plan on a large calendar in the library and staff room. With this tool in place, especially in larger settings, the teacher-librarian may not work with every teacher but hopefully with all the students and for adequate periods of time. For example, if the English and math teachers are involved in most projects, all students will still benefit. What will develop over time with this strategy is an information literacy continuum for the school. This ensures program continuity in information literacy for the students over time, as well as incorporates new students or staff into the process, such as demonstrated in the example of what this continuum might look like, K–12, in chapter 5 of this book. What might a long-range brain friendly school library calendar plan look like?

Primary

September—Library orientation, all 10 classrooms; Grade 2/3, Science and Lit in the Garden study; Grade 4, Adventure novels to complement "Weather & Natural Forces" study

October—Grade 1/2, Alphabet centres "Finding Authors"; Grade 4, Community of Readers workshops

November—Kindergarten, Illustrator study; Grade 3, History project

December—Grade 2/3, "Dewey" project in conjunction with winter unit

January–February—Grade 4, Natural resources inquiry; Grade 3, Author study

March–April—Grade 3, Reading/writing workshops; Grade 1, Plant research

May–June—Grade 4 and Kindergarten, Collective inquiry into "family" topic; Grade 2, Music and building structures project

Middle School

September—Library orientation, all 20 classrooms; Grade 9, Latin America inquiry; Grade 6, Mystery novels to complement forensic science unit

October—Grade 8, Ecosystem inquiry; Grade 5, Community of Readers workshops

November—Grade 7, Art class illustrator study; Grade 5, Civic history project

December—Grade 9, Poetry study to complement History unit

January–February—Grade 6, Ancient civilizations inquiry; Grade 7, Community of Readers

March–April—Grade 5, Reading/writing workshops; Grade 9, Math and art project

May–June—Grade 8 and Grade 9, Collective inquiry into "How advertising affects lifestyle" topic; Grade 6, History and dance project

High School

September—Orientation for all English classes to the library; Character project begins—each student will present a character from literature in choice of representation: visual art, drama (come as the character), video, PowerPoint

October–November—Grade 10, Humanities inquiry; Grade 11, Biology classes working with arts department on cellular study, Fashion Studies inquiry into art history and fashion, Math 30 exit project action research planning begins for June Math project fair

December—Math 30 students continue project, English classes celebrate "character week" with art, drama, projects displayed

January–February—Science 10 students study and recreate versions of *12 Angry Men* to produce own rap versions of Scopes monkey trial in study of evolution, Math students continue action research

March–April—"Physics" then and now project begins with historical look at physics concepts dating back to Leonardo Da Vinci, Interview current physicists to understand how physics relates to life today, Math students continue action research

May–June—Civics students create dioramas that show improvements to local problem areas, meet with city officials to present, Math project fair held involving local businesses

Many school libraries have moved or are moving in this direction to bring inquiry and research to new, deeper life and meaning for students and teachers in brain friendly practices. Users do not collect and disseminate data but become information literate evaluators, analysers, and creators as school libraries move from "controlling" resources to becoming learning laboratories. What can brain friendly action research using interdisciplinary teams look like across the grades? It involves the student as researcher, scientist, investigator, and explorer. It is relevant and experiential. Here follow three of the suggested inquiry/action research projects mentioned in the calendars above in greater detail.

Primary: Science and Literature in the Garden

- Begin with a problem: "The school courtyard is ugly—old concrete with patches of weeds. How would you, the students, make it more beautiful?"
- Students use graphic organizers to state past knowledge: Students create mind maps (Web) with the problem in the centre and all the ideas they can generate on how to make the courtyard more beautiful surrounding the topic.
- Students form questions: Have students generate a few good questions relating to their mind maps. For example, if they want to plant flowers— What types of flowers grow best here? What type of soil is needed? How will we care for them?
- Students decide on the scope of their context: Will they redesign the whole space? Certain sections? Who will they need help from? Where can they find information? Add these to the Web.
- Decide on one main issue to focus on: Plants? Trees? Soil? Paint? What will it be?
- Resources: Students should be able to access and share many fictional picture books on beautifying spaces and gardens such as Timothy Ering's *The Story of Frog Belly Rat Bone* (2003). Nonfiction garden and plant books and Internet sources can be introduced here to garner more information on their quests. Remind them to make notes and diagrams from their "literature search" and also note titles and authors for a basic bibliography.
- Goals, outcomes, action plans: Now that they are more informed on their ideas, have the students focus on a goal they would like to develop further such as a "boxed vegetable garden" in the courtyard. Have them decide on an outcome—vegetables for soup—and create a plan of action.
- Journey: Conducting the plan of action may include interviewing experts—the local greenhouse manager or a parent who gardens. It will involve writing key questions to which answers are needed to proceed ahead with the idea.

- Patterns/themes: Have students reflect on their "journey." What new things did they learn? For example, did they discover what plants are hardiest? Did they think about the possibility of vandalism?
- Conclusion: Have the students decide how they wish to represent their discoveries. On a poster? A model? A diorama? Will the class transform the courtyard?

Middle School: Art/Illustrator Study

- Begin with a problem: How will the study of a variety of children's book illustrators impact my work as an artist?
- Students use graphic organizers to state past knowledge: Students create charts with suggested categories for generating ideas on what they know or can recall about picture book art. Colour: Bright? Dull? Style: Cartoonish? Realistic? Humorous? Pretty? Composition: Flat? Layers? Technique: Watercolour? Pencil and ink? Title: Do they recall any favourite books?
- Students form questions: Have students generate a few good questions relating to their charts. For example, who illustrates picture books? Why would anyone want to? Why would it matter to my art? What can I learn from picture books?
- Students decide on the scope of their context: Will they study one author? Five? A larger selection? Time periods in picture book art? Images or themes and how they have been illustrated? For example, dragons. Who will they need help from? Where can they find information? Add these to the Web.
- Decide on one main issue to focus on: "The five most recent Caldecott winners"; animal stories.
- Resources: Students should be able to access and share many picture books, particularly noting the many picture books published recently that really are for an older reader. Nonfiction books and Internet sources come into play here to garner more information on their quests. Remind them to make notes and diagrams from their "literature search" and also note titles and authors for a basic bibliography.
- Goals, outcomes, action plans: Now that they are more informed on their ideas, have the students focus on a goal they would like to develop further, such as "realism in picture book illustrations." Have them decide on an outcome—a picture book for a younger student—and create a plan of action.
- Journey: Conducting the plan of action may include interviewing experts such as illustrators either locally or through their Web sites. It will involve writing key questions for which answers are needed to proceed ahead with the study.
- Patterns/themes: Have students reflect on their "journey." What new things did they learn? For example, did they discover how they could be influenced as an artist by their choice of study?
- Conclusion: Have the students decide how they wish to present their discoveries. On a poster? A model? A picture book of their own? A painting trying a new style?

High School: Math Project Fair

- Begin with a problem: How will you demonstrate to members of the local business community the relevance and applicability of a chosen project in advanced mathematics study?

- Students use graphic organizers to state past knowledge: Students create flow charts with the problem in the centre and all the ideas they can generate on how to make advanced math relevant to business.

- Students form questions: Have students generate a few good questions relating to their flow chart. For example, could I create a better way of analysing stock investments? Would an engineering problem be solved based on a mathematical formula?

- Students decide on the scope of their context: Will they focus on one local business (a bank)? Or study the stock market? Will they look at marketing trends across the nation or for their jurisdiction in predicting a new product's success?

- Decide on one main issue to focus on: The issue will be one that enables the student to share the beauty of math with its practical applicability in realms of business, science, and art.

- Resources: Students should be able to access and share a variety of sources from a variety of libraries, real (university?), and online. Remind them to make notes and diagrams from their "literature search" and also note titles and authors for a basic bibliography.

- Goals, outcomes, action plans: Now that they are more informed on their ideas, have the students focus on a goal they would like to develop further, such as a market prediction analysis for a new software product. Have them decide on an outcome—presenting to a local software firm and bank—and create a plan of action.

- Journey: Conducting the plan of action may include interviewing experts—university professors, businesspeople, scientists, mathematicians. It will involve writing key questions for which answers are needed to proceed ahead with the idea.

- Patterns/themes: Have students reflect on their "journey." What new things did they learn? For example, did they discover practical applications for the math topic chosen? Did they think about other possibilities?

- Conclusion: Have the students decide how they wish to present their discoveries on project day. In a display? A model? A PowerPoint demo? A commercial? Have visiting experts or businesspeople judge the most viable projects.

Chapter 10

INFORMATION LITERACY

"Information literacy" suggests or can mean the coming to terms with one's own thinking. For an individual of this media-packaged century, understanding and developing one's own learning is a huge challenge. It is more the ability to "know how to learn" that is vital in our society than the random memorization of facts deemed important by interest groups of the past. There arise certain backlashes to this, in the appearance of "back to basics" schools and programs, but defining "basics," particularly in a brain friendly school library environment, is open to debate and should be.

Being information literate—indeed, "learning how to learn"—builds neural connections in our brains. Learning and relearning keeps the brain active: The brain wants to make order out of chaos; it seeks patterns. The brain accesses input, evaluates it, and uses information from many sources for our basic survival to our most advanced thinking. As mentioned earlier in chapter 3 on Bob Sylwester's work, the library is a good metaphor for the function of the brain. These attributes of accessing data, evaluating it, analysing it, and applying it form the foundations of both the American Association of School Libraries' "Information Power" and the Canadian School Library Association's "Achieving Information Literacy." These processes are foundational to teacher-librarians' study and practice, yet they must take them far beyond their realm to permeate classroom practice and curricular relevance, with the school library as focal point—going beyond its "walls" and letting the world come into it.

Information literacy sometimes pins itself to a limited picture of the worlds of library or English class—books, newspapers, periodicals, the Internet, the odd unit on advertising or television, and so on. Thinking about the term must expand, as was so aptly documented by Linda Langford in her article "Information Literacy: A Clarification" (1998), to think in terms of a multiplicity of literacies—numeric, cultural, political, scientific, media, traditional, and more.

Becoming more multiliterate, or aware of the various ways to express, understand, and create meaning, will require ways of reading and thinking beyond words in books to processes required for reading and thinking in all formats. Importantly, in many areas, time and dollars have been devoted to "early literacy" for good reason. Yet it seems as though the time and dollars stopped once basic text was assumed mastered. There can often be a lack of transference from "basic" early literacy skills to later literature, reading of the Internet, and film. By taking a factual definition of the term "information literacy" as "the ability to access, evaluate, and use information from a variety of sources," many questions need to be considered by teacher-librarians, teachers, and students. Do we take the time to learn to "read" what is being communicated in a piece of artwork? An artefact? A dance? A graphic novel? A symphony or rap song? A math equation? A video or film? Television? Statistics abound with the number of hours children, and adults, spend looking at television or surfing the Net, yet schools of the twenty-first century largely ignore this subliminal intrusion into our collective psyche and culture.

The school library has played, and will continue to play, a key role in brain friendly practices around information literacy. Any type of literacy harkens back to the brain's biological cycle of input, analysis, action, and reflection—tenets of evaluation used traditionally in developing library or museum collections. These tenets form the foundations of metacognition—the literate person being one who can objectively evaluate and debate the choice of a book, a film, a painting, a Web site. Why is evaluation left to reviewers, journalists, arts critics, movie critics, and marketers? Each student must hone and develop information literacy basics to deal with the amount and types of information our brains are bombarded within today's global world. How might some information literacy projects look across the grades?

Primary: What Is Good? Judging Video

Begin planning as early as kindergarten with the kindergarten teachers. Continue yearly, developing a continuum that continues with "What makes a good video?" "What makes a good Web site?" "Art piece?" And so on, depending on the needs of students and teachers.

Using a selection of primary videos, brainstorm with students what they think the criteria for a "good film" are. How will they "judge"? Include some award winners. Set up cooperative groups to explore the material, discuss likes and dislikes.

From the brainstorm, categorise words the students have generated into like categories.

The following categories should arise or may need to be taught in mini-lessons surrounding this study. It is important to co-generate subcategory questions to further thinking around the concepts.

New or old? (Currency)

    How can you tell when it was made?

    What clues are in the pictures? Words? Actions?

    Is the topic something we find important or still talk about?

Fun or boring? (Relevance)

True or false? (Accuracy—particularly with nonfiction)

Beautiful or ugly? (Aesthetics)

Easy to use or too hard to understand? (Accessibility)

Could be enjoyed by everyone? (Bias, objectivity, not condescending)

Post the words you decide to use and use them in other studies and when students are independently selecting books as well as other resources.

Middle School: What Is Best? Comparing Form

This idea would work best with the English or humanities teachers.

Engage students in a study of a literary work that can be shared in a variety of formats, such as Dr. Seuss's *How the Grinch Stole Christmas*—first presented as a children's storybook, then an animated version (televised yearly), then a full-length feature film with all the marketing attached, currently televised yearly or owned by many families.

Have students in groups create charts for the three formats—children's book/animated feature/full-length film. Have them brainstorm criteria for how they will judge each type of media. Share with the class—come to consensus on the terminology. Most of the terms the students generate should match these standards. The standard terms should be used and posted on a continuous basis such as in the example below.

Picture Book	*Animated Feature*	*Film*
Current?	Current?	Current?
Relevant? (to you)	Relevant?	Relevant?
Accurate/Authentic? / Who wrote it?	Accurate/Authentic? Who adapted it?	Accurate/Authentic? Who adapted it? Directed?
Aesthetic? Pleasing? Artistic?	Aesthetic? Pleasing? Artistic?	Aesthetic? Pleasing? Artistic?
Accessible—ease of use?	Accessible—ease of use?	Accessible—ease of use?
Durable?	Durable?	Durable?
Appeal to all? Bias present?	Appeal to all? Bias present?	Appeal to all? Bias present?

    After students read or view each selection, groups should return to charts or tables to discuss the format details.

Picture Book	*Animated Feature*	*Film*
Current? Look at the details in the pictures. How can you tell when it was made? What are other clues?	Current? Study the artwork. How does it compare to today's animated features?	Current? What has changed here in the look of the film? Its design?
Relevant? (to you) Does this work say or mean anything to you now? When you were younger?	Relevant? How will watching it in this form change the meaning for you or others? Will it?	Relevant? This is a much longer version—does this change the meaning? Why or why not?
Accurate/Authentic? Is this the original?	Accurate/Authentic? What has changed from the original work?	Accurate/Authentic? What has further changed from the original?
Aesthetic? Pleasing? Artistic? What makes a picture book "good"? How does this compare?	Aesthetic? Pleasing? Artistic? What makes an "animation" good? How does this compare?	Aesthetic? Pleasing? Artistic? What makes a film "good"? How does this compare?
Accessible—ease of use? Durable?	Accessible—ease of use? Durable?	Accessible—ease of use? Durable?
Appeal to all? Bias present?	Appeal to all? Bias present?	Appeal to all? Bias present?

Students should now be able to share their findings and opinions in a variety of ways. Some students may prefer the book, others the film or animation. This could be presented setting up a "television set"; then have the students videotape as "reviewers."

High School: What Is Real? Sorting Out the "Chaos"

- A science or English class may work best for this information literacy project's theme where students are exploring a controversial issue such as cloning, stem cell research, or current world situations. Some high school students will have been taught or have developed evaluative skills. Others may never have or have not processed them into long-term memory, for whatever reason. It is still wise to have students generate evaluative qualities of a variety of media formats (using a table or chart similar to the one previously presented).

- Students will be asked to determine how a person can tell if information is factual or contrived. They will be seeking to understand authority/authenticity as a major focus to their work while learning or relearning other evaluative criteria. It may be pointed out that although the "media" have manipulated data historically—"spin doctors" abound in early civilizations—today the average citizen can manipulate data with increasing effectiveness. For example, Casio of Japan has developed a digital camera that can blend two photos without the need for a personal computer: When the "combined" button is pushed, the camera's software "stitches" the two pictures together by correcting colour and contrast mismatches.

- Student findings on their topics could be presented as a debate, mock trial, or documentary video.

Chapter 11

PROJECTS

Project- and problem-based learning are natural to brain friendly activities and school library learning. Many school library learning experiences are framed as projects or have been in preceding chapters. This chapter takes the focus to another level important to brain friendly learning—where project- or problem-based learning focuses less on instructor-contrived projects and more on problems, projects, or simulations directly related to the students they are teaching, their issues, or the local community. Although all types of school library experiences need to connect with students' understanding of the world, and indeed to broaden it with new concepts or knowledge to reflect on, project-based learning in this sense is much more focused on a direct reality.

Many teachers are embracing this pedagogy in the classroom, and there are a great number of Web sites and Web quests to consult in this area. A good example is the "WebQuest Page" of San Diego University (http://webquest.sdsu.edu). This is an excellent tool for the teacher-librarian's study and use while collaboratively project planning with a teacher. These types of projects are constructivist or generative in nature, letting the students take the lead in expanding or changing activities as they contribute, plan, reason, listen, and design.

Projects can become exhibitions or vehicles for formal disciplinary work; they can indeed become disciplinary showcases. They demonstrate direct application, experience, and relevance in understanding curriculum and making school meaningful. Projects permit students to work within their preferred intellectual learning styles, allowing them and others to compare how other students and staff make meaning of the world. Projects facilitate collaboration; students can see that in real-life situations all may not agree, but all must strive to build consensus: This builds brain power. Project-based learning in this sense is based on problem-based learning, starting with or incorporating a real-time issue or problem to work on, and is often very practical and service oriented, for example, protecting a local ecological area. These types of projects will make the school and school library more visible and viable in the community.

Often after a series of school and school library projects the teachers will request more of this kind of realistic focus on the work collaboratively planned with the teacher-librarian. Where time or budget constraints make it not possible to always have the teacher-librarian present, a plan could be devised where teacher teams carry on with collaboratively planned projects with a same-grade teacher, cross-divisional teacher, or another subject teacher having learned the skills necessary from working with the teacher-librarian.

Project-based learning in this sense generates projects that are real and that take time but make a difference in the actual lives of the students. A large project of this nature can involve achieving many subject area goals and skills using brain friendly principles of relevancy and experiential learning. These projects will demonstrate to students the importance of reading in all formats, writing, analysing, and researching in many ways, and applying math and science. These are the projects most remembered and treasured. What can these projects look like involving the school library as a focal point?

Primary: Nutrition and the Brain

- It is never too early for learners to develop metacognition around how their brains work and what is best for health and learning.
- The planning team can focus on the health, science, and language arts curricula. Their goal is to make recommendations to the school through creating posters and "public service" announcements pertaining to "brain health." Check with the school office to see when students can make the announcements, place posters. Additionally, students may generate project ideas of their own, for example, holding weekly nutrition contests such as "Fresh Fruit Fridays" and tallying which classes brought the most fruit products for snack.
- Easy nonfiction sources (books, videos, Web sites) are available and will need to be on hand for the research component of the project. Three "stations" can be set up with three different types of note-taking strategies— diagrams from books, electronic webbing from the Internet (e.g., Inspiration program), key phrases from a video.
- The teacher-librarian and teacher can help students summarize the key points of their findings.
- Students can work independently or in pairs to create their posters/ announcements. Skills relating to posters/announcements/citing reference sources will need to be taught along with rubrics designed for assessment.
- Students may wish to use a survey before and after their project to see if any of their recommended changes occurred; then discuss why or why not. For example, in two schools a vote was made by the student body to remove the pop machine and replace soda pop with juice and water. In another, water bottles were encouraged on all desks. In another, the school library purchased more resources on the topic including starting a "parent library" with such resources.

Middle School: Seedfolks/Food Bank Project

- *Seedfolks*, Paul Fleischman's Newberry Award–winning book (1997), can become an ideal novel study to inspire community action around environmental and social issues.
- This can involve the English teacher as well as the science teacher.
- The teacher or teacher-librarian may wish to present the novel by reading each short, succinct chapter, then have the students dialogue about the characters in small groups and sketch portraits of the characters for a library "art gallery."
- Science research groups can be established to have the students focus in on an applicable project from the study. Projects could range from designing and growing an indoor garden (herb) within the school or school library to developing a school garden where each class plants a section in the school yard. The latter project would involve working with the administration in the school and the school board, learning about the soil and types of plants that will grow, creating a purpose: Will the garden supply fresh produce for the school cafeteria? The food bank? Local families? Perhaps there is an area in the community better suited to a community garden. How will students work to make that happen?

High School: Substance Abuse—Preserving Brain Health

- This is similar in design to the primary project but focusing on brain health at a much more complex level and pertinent to issues concerning teen learners. As in other aspects of background, students may have some awareness of metacognition, health, and the brain; others will be at novice stages.
- The planning team can focus on health, science (biology), or English curricula. The goal is to raise awareness around personal health decisions relating to "brain health and substance abuse."
- Inquiry groups, stations, teams, or individuals can be set up with up to ten different types of note-taking strategies/resources—diagrams from books, electronic webbing from the Internet (e.g., Inspiration program), key phrases from a video, tape recording from an "expert" in the area, chart summarizing various periodical views on the issue (paper and electronic), survey from the student body, note cards from science/health technical books, and so on.
- From the research, students will need assistance to analyse their data for patterns, themes, and conclusions.
- Students can work independently or in pairs to decide how they will share their findings and recommendations to make an impact on teen choice around substance use. Reference skills relating to their choice of medium may need to be taught along with rubrics designed for assessment. If students wish to create professional-looking posters, the art or design teacher may become involved at this stage. If they want to write and perform a play, the English and drama teacher. If they want to create a PowerPoint presentation, the teacher-librarian.
- Each of the ways of sharing should produce or suggest a result that could be voted on and discussed with school administration. For example, someone might suggest removing the "smoking pit" or adding a vending

machine that sells healthier products. Perhaps a "drug information line" is set up through a student radio station or a parent/teen talk night arranged around issues.

• Depending on the sophistication of the student/staff body in representational learning, the planning team may decide on a small variety of project expressions and teach those or have the students branch out more, depending on their base skill level.

• Students may wish to create an attitudinal survey pre and post their projects to see if any of their recommendations changed attitude/practices, then discuss why or why not.

Part IV

GOAL 3: EMOTIONAL ENVIRONMENTS— TEACHER-LIBRARIAN AS CULTURAL EMISSARY

Making more brain friendly emotional connections to literature, arts, and sciences will enhance memory and learning of cultural heritage.

The achievement of this goal will involve more sensory experiences, cooperative learning, and reflection/celebration.

Chapter 12

SENSORY LEARNING—LITERATURE AND THE ARTS

Sensory learning focuses on the fact that it is through our senses that the brain receives input from the environment, and the process of interpreting, analysing, and using the input is engaged. Schools traditionally focus on visual perception in learning and representation of learning. Sensory learning, prevalent in advancements in studying and representing the arts, can be highly effective in engaging students in other curricular learning and deepening of understanding. It allows the student to look at things from varying perspective. It broadens the educator's view on assessment: No one would take an artist or actor into a room and give him or her a test; the individual would perform, based on a long-established criteria. For at least 2,000 years, known criteria have been used successfully in critiquing the arts, even athletics, but not other disciplines.

Learning and teaching through the arts—visual art, music, drama, dance, and literature—leads us into the area of critique and sensory exploration. Exploration into any of the art forms including multisensory entry points can be lively fodder for creating neural pathways. Imagine looking at a painting and hearing music, or hearing music to create a sculpture. All speak to a basic human quality—story. From oral stories to the great operas or novels of time, the human story is played out. Literature and the arts have been key components of school libraries and their programs. A wonderful piece of literature can make us see, feel, smell, taste, and hear a story that resonates within our soul or takes us somewhere else, letting us experience familiar or unfamiliar emotions. Reading literature keeps the brain nourished and growing.

Teacher-librarians should be known for their vitally important role in developing literacy in the traditional sense of reading literature. Although the notion of literacy can be expanded to include many formats, the focus that students, staff, and the public have often valued is the expertise of the teacher-librarian in children's and young adult literature. The teacher-librarian's role as "the book person" has been trodden upon as critics pipe up about the "demise of books" and as technology and other media take over, bombarding the senses with quick info bites rather than the joy offered through the slower reflective reading of a book. Based purely on local public library usage and growth, and the international growth of bookstore chains such as Chapters, Indigo, Barnes and Noble, and Amazon, "books" in today's world flourish more than ever. The publishing industry is booming, and books are more readily available, more beautifully made, and more treasured than ever before.

Ultimately, it will not matter what "form" books appear in: Most people still like to "curl up" in bed or on the sofa with a paper book, even if someday it might appear as a "hologram" floating near our eyes via some technological device; the electronic book promised on the market really has not taken off yet. What does matter, and should matter more, is that children and young adult teacher-librarians have a vast background experience with excellent literature for young people. In some parts of the world, teacher-librarians have been "downsized" from schools as movements such as "early literacy" and technology have reconfigured literacy to a basic set of words or programs or software. Studies reveal that without a teacher-librarian, literacy scores soon plummet downward, no matter what type of literacy "program" is in vogue in the school. Who else but the teacher-librarian has read all (or many) of the books in the library?

The teacher-librarian's expertise in bringing young learners and faculty into the culture of great literature, past and present, has thus been in recent times overlooked. Within the heart of any country's or culture's literature beats the mores, patterns, and customs of that civilization. Great truths such as the battle between good and evil are played out on many stages and with many characters in every language. Teacher-librarians have studied this vast collective cultural heritage in depth. It translates itself into many user questions that cannot be answered easily if that expertise is not available. Do these basic questions sound familiar?

"Can you help me find a dog story?"

"I'm new on staff—what novels would go with my unit on adventure?"

"My students seem to be stuck on one type of book—what would inspire them to read more?

"Where is that funny book about hats?"

"I loved *Lord of the Rings*. I cried in certain parts. Are there other books like that?"

"I hate reading! But I have to get a book for a book report. Help!"

"I need 50 picture books, videos, and some art prints for an art study on illustration techniques."

"I'm ready for a chapter book!"

And if there is not a teacher-librarian? Do some of the newer teachers even ask these questions? Who assists the children, especially the large majority who are not using the public library? Who sets up links to public libraries? To the worlds of the imagination? To finding books that exemplify excellence to those worlds?

Following are ideas for literature projects that are also multisensory in nature. By engaging the students and staff in this way, it is hoped that over time the information literacy continuum in the school will hold place for students (and teachers) to develop a larger base of knowledge of children's/young adult authors, genres, and styles in the great realm of children's/young adult literature. In assisting teachers, the teacher-librarian could use literature, or any of the arts, as a starting point for planning, regardless of the subject.

Primary

Bug-o-ramas: Students explore the miniature worlds of insects through arts and the senses in order to create a bug-o-rama (diorama that incorporates all the senses from an insect point of view). Therefore, an ant bug-o-rama would have a visual of the habitat, a jar of honey to taste, leaves or dirt to touch and smell, a tape recording or other sound device created as to what an ant might hear (rustling leaves, loud footsteps, etc.).

Exploration:

Sight:

Read and share a variety of fiction on bugs such as the *Miss Spider* series.

Provide nonfiction books on insects.

Provide famous paintings incorporating bugs or study illustrations from picture books.

Look at videos of insect life or Internet sites containing video clips.

If possible, examine lapidary collections under glass.

Touch:

Depending on the season, bugs can be "caught" (gently and safely) on the field and very gently touched—for example, a grasshopper, a caterpillar.

Sculptures, models, or toy bugs can be used.

Bug environmental features to touch: leaves, grass, dirt.

Have students mime or create movement relating to how they observe/perceive the movements of bugs.

Create "bug sculptures" in groups where one student is the head, another the wings, another the legs, and so on.

Taste:

While reading fiction, ask the students to imagine what bug food tastes like.

Items that are safe to taste could be brought in—for example, honey, certain grasses, seeds.

Smell:

Mystery jars: put common elements (leaves, dirt, etc.) into unlabeled, covered jars and have students guess what they are by smell.

Have students imagine smells inherent in stories about bugs.

Sound:

Listen to music or songs about bugs.

Imagine and create "soundtracks" for one of the bug stories.

Create big and little sounds—what we sound like to bugs and what their world would sound like to us.

Middle School

Literary Character Chamber: Students create sensory collage masks of favourite characters from junior fiction for the library "gallery." Masks can be made using plaster of paris and student faces to mould in conjunction with the art or drama teacher. Masks will be decorated with fine felts, paints, and glued-on images to reflect key sensory attributes of the character chosen. They will divide their mask into five areas—an area around the eyes, mouth, and nose, the cheek areas close to the ears, and the forehead, symbolizing touch, feeling.

Exploration:

Sight:

Individually or in groups (reader's workshop) students choose novels from a selection provided that introduce new and classic characters—for example, "Bilbo Baggins," "Harry Potter or Hermione," "Maurice" (*Maurice and the Educated Rats*), "Jonas or The Giver," Alex (*Skinnybones*), and so on.

Materials on mask design and collage are provided—books, Web sites, actual examples, if possible.

Students choose how they will illustrate the character's sight area: Will they draw or paint glasses on (Harry Potter?) or go to the more symbolic such as writing words around Jonas's eyes to tell what he has been shown a sled, Christmas, and so on?

Touch:

Mask making is very tactile. Once completed, have students decide on how they will portray the forehead (touch, feelings) of the character. Painted or drawn images? Glued-on pictures to collage? "Wrinkles" for The Giver?

Taste:

How will the character's mouth be depicted? For example, will "Maurice" be "eating" a mouse? Will Alex be eating more cereal?

Smell:

What will the nose depict? A pine tree as Bilbo walks through the forest?

Sound:

The area of the cheeks of the mask near the ears depicts sound—will this be a collage of words? Symbols?

High School

Installation Art: Students present story of Margaret Atwood's *Oryx and Crate* (2003) through a series of installation pieces throughout the library and the school.

After reading the novel, students in groups prepare a storyboard outlining important scenes from the novel.

Each group is assigned or chooses one scene to work on. Visitors or other students may follow a "map" of the pieces to follow the story.

Books, videos, and Web sites on art installation are made available/taught for study of the medium.

Exploration:

    Sight:

        Each installation piece has visual elements—this is like building a set for a play.

    Touch:

        Each installation should include a feature that is tactile either in viewing it or being able to touch it.

    Taste:

        Each installation should include a feature related to taste or involving food from the book.

    Smell:

        Students can include materials or devices that engage the sense of smell, such as perfume or air freshers that smell like forests, the sea, or a symbolic smell such as vanilla.

    Sound:

        Elements of sound incorporated into the installation can be tape-recorded voices or songs, nature sounds, drumbeats—whatever works with the chosen scene.

Chapter 13

COOPERATIVE LEARNING—COLLABORATIVE PLANNING AND TEACHING

An emotionally enriched environment is one in which working together is valued and respect for diversity is cherished. What better model to demonstrate productive teamwork in action than the cooperative planning model involving teachers and a teacher-librarian? This practice has allowed teacher-librarians to become leaders in information literacy in school programs and projects. It has expanded the teacher-librarian's role as cultural facilitator into a leader in learning and a resource for all subject areas and new instructional methodologies. The methodology of cooperative learning (Kagan 1990) must also be structured into school library learning experiences and co-created for the students by the teacher-librarian and teachers.

The brain thrives on working with other brains, desiring feedback, and cooperative learning methodology provides much of that from teacher or peer—coaching, guiding, socializing, being recognized as emotional beings, accepted, and influential. This methodology provides positive, dendrite-growing responses to the often-dreaded concept of "group work." According to noted educator Alfie Kohn (1991), "[C]arefully structured cooperative learning promotes a subjective sense of group identity, a greater acceptance of people who are different from oneself (in terms of ethnicity or ability level), and a more sophisticated ability to imagine other people's points of view." This "group" or collective critical thinking leads to skills in judgmental maturity. Students learn to become more moral and ethically capable as collective thinkers and beings.

The brain is a social brain, and we are social beings. Some blame the "industrial age" and its factory models, but students have largely ended up in desks and rows, regurgitating so-called basic facts, and having their silence lauded as a virtue. Even more so, libraries were quiet study halls, with dusty shelves filled with tomes of knowledge. Yet learning in the social experience defines collaboration and makes school student's authentic "work." Students question each other, help each other, find out what others think, explain, learn how to listen better, do things on their own, show others how to do things, make up their own minds, strive for consensus, contribute, give reasons for ideas, pull ideas together, and apply learning to develop a plan or strategy.

Cooperative learning groups must be structured carefully with clear written or oral instructions, activities that students can complete with a degree of independence, and put the teacher and teacher-librarian in the role of facilitator. Cooperative groups develop trust over a month to six-week period and work best in fours. Groups can be created randomly, using a class mixer–type activity, or heterogeneously, depending on your needs and purpose. Cooperative groups allow a mix of learner-style activities and multisensory/intelligence approaches. Cooperative learning supports democratic education: Students provide direct or indirect feedback on each other's learning and the teacher/school/teacher-librarian planning. Questions formed lead to additional enrichment or discoveries by students and often let students take the lead in expanding or changing activities. Ongoing consulting and debriefing with groups is critical to the process, checking perceptions with individuals to address issues or concerns. Groups are not disbanded if problems occur; students must work together to figure out successful solutions.

This approach revisualizes school library "activities" or skills into a more process-oriented library learning center or "library centers," using the cooperative planning model with teachers and cooperative learning strategies with students. Learners use collections of materials to explore topics or practice skills relating to information literacy. They engage as active learners, incorporating resources in information-rich environments and effectively using them. Over time, the demand for the library centers leads to an information literacy continuum developing over the school. Many of these centers were published in the book *Library Centers* (Sykes 1997), and new centers are created yearly with new teachers.

Teachers enjoy the creative planning process and look freshly at using the library and addressing information literacy in ways they know will engage the students. Planning, implementing, and evaluating instructional activities jointly lead to much professional growth. Teachers are challenged to attempt diverse methodology, build upon current modes of practice, and give learners a greater amount/variety of experiences with resources.

Students repeatedly look forward to these centers, continually revised based on student/teacher need and emerging technology. Students state that they enjoy working at their own pace in situations involving their peers. They benefit from the socialization and group culture, shared creativity, shared responsibilities with materials, reading instructions, and tasks. They can receive coaching or guidance easily from the teacher or teacher-librarian or peers. They can discuss, dialogue, and debate as they interact with resources. Students become more than independent lifelong learners; they become codependent, collaborative team players. In many cases, the classroom programs do not provide a lot of time for building these essential attributes and skills; the school library can offer this model in collaborative planning and teaching, thus leading the way into structuring highly effective social and emotional brain-rich experiences.

The teacher-librarian and teacher or teaching teams must establish norms of groups with students and often teach cooperative and social skills, asking, "How do we want our school library groups to be?" Other adults in the learning community can be included for student benefit, depending on the nature and complexity of the centers. Library assistants or technicians often assist and appreciate being able to share their expertise with small groups of students at a time such as in centers for locating materials from an OPAC or finding books on the shelves. University students, parents, administrators, resource personnel, community guests, and online experts can be involved with cooperative learning centers. Topics that lend themselves well for development as school library centers include interpretation of literature, humanities, or science programs. Again, the ideas, talents, and interests of the planning team will determine how such work would look at a school. Following are samples of possibilities for brain friendly "library centers" focusing on expanding the student repertoire of knowing a variety of authors and incorporating the arts.

Primary: "ABC Centers"

This library learning experience reinforces the concept of alphabetization in primary language learning and applying those skills to finding picture books in the library based on "author's last name." It introduces a wide variety of authors to the students.

These five centers are designed for a class of twenty to twenty-five, with four to five students in a group. The school/teacher-librarian teaches one group, and it is encouraged to have the library assistant/technician involved in another, and three other volunteers booked for the other centers (parents, administrators?).

Center One: OPAC

Facilitated by the teacher-librarian or library assistant.

Have the group share their surnames and each take a turn to enter his or her own surname into the OPAC; some will discover authors with last names similar to their own.

Hand each student a popular picture book and have each type in the author's last name; when it appears—for example, Carle, Eric—point out the location of the call letter ("C"—picture book authors) and take the student to the shelf.

Continue with the others, making the connection with the OPAC and location on the shelf.

Center Two: Shelf Work

Facilitated by the teacher-librarian or library assistant.

Make five sets of five large (8×11 inch) coloured, laminated cards with authors' names—last name first, and first letter of last name underlined: for example, <u>C</u>ARLE, Eric.

Have each student put his or her set in alphabetic order by the author's last name, students helping each other and coached by the adult.

Have the students go to the shelves to find the author and mark the place with the card.

Center Three: Plastecine ABCs

Assign each student a letter.

Have an assortment of picture books at the center with illustrators who use plastecine, for example, Barbara Reid.

Have 8×11 inch cardboard panels cut.

Have the student make the letter out of plastecine and create an image out of plastecine to represent the letter: for example, Apple for A.

Display the alphabet in the library "gallery."

Center Four: Alphabet Authors

Have a selection of picture books by a variety of authors/illustrators that depict the alphabet: everything from Kate Greenaway's *A Apple Pie* (1978) or Tasha Tudor's *A is for Annabelle* (1954) to Denise Fleming's *Alphabet Under Construction* (2002).

Enjoy looking at and exploring the various takes on the alphabet.

Each student can decide how he or she would like to express the alphabet and create a first page for his or her own alphabet book. (Teachers may want to have some or all of the students continue and make a whole alphabet book.)

Center Five: My First Dictionary

Have a selection of junior dictionaries with five sets of ten recipe-type cards with words printed on them.

Have students alphabetize their set and use the dictionaries to find the words, marking the place with the card; the adult at the station can point out basic dictionary skills.

Trade word card sets as students complete the set.

Middle School: "Author Jeopardy"

Having students select and read their own novels and have their own authors to research—the purpose being that students will be exposed to junior literature, enhancing oral and written communication skills, and literary discussion in brain friendly groups.

Organize the students into groups of four or five and assign facilitators to centers as available.

Have students rotate through the centers, where they will be gaining more information and discussion about their novels for the ultimate purpose of creating an "Author Jeopardy" game.

After the centers are complete, groups will create game cards based on the categories of the centers (author data, plot lines, characters, setting locations, novel research topics) and organize an "Author Jeopardy" tournament. The tournament could be videotaped, with all the sound effects, and have invited "guests" to judge.

Center One: Author Email

Have students use Internet sources to research the author of their novel.

Have them use a brainstorming software tool such as "Inspiration" to create an "author Web" document using key words from the author's site.

Have the students compose and send an email to the author (or publisher if the author is deceased), giving an opinion of the novel and requesting information not found on the author's Web site.

Center Two: Character Creation

Have the students select their favourite character from the novel.

Have the students decide which modern actor/actress would best play the part of that character if the novel were to be filmed.

Have the students create news interviews with the actor/actress, asking them ten questions about the character role they are playing from the novel. Conduct the interviews within the teams.

Center Three: Location, Location

Have the students record the setting(s), time, and place of their novels.

Let the students choose an artistic representation of the setting (to be later displayed in the library): watercolour, sketch, pastel, other.

Center Four: Novel Research

Have the students choose a factual subject from their book that the author had to research to write it (e.g., *Shiloh*, West Virginia; beagles). Request that they research the subject, briefly, from two sources and create a short report with diagram about the topic.

Center Five: Plot Graphs

Have students create "plot graphs" of their novels showing the events of the story (beginning, rising action, climax, denouement).

Illustrate the "graphs" using cartoon style.

High School: "Discovering Authors and Genres"

These centers promote high school English students learning about more authors and genres than the standard "novel" usually taught as part of the English course or the genre that forms their traditional comfort zone (i.e., "horror books").

Organize the students into groups of five and assign facilitators to centers as needed/available. In the example, I have chosen five genres for a class of twenty-five; you may need to create more genre-based centers, depending on class size.

Select a variety of new and classic novels from the genres to be highlighted and have bibliographies available at each center for the students, along with succinct information describing the genre characteristics.

Have students rotate through the centers for the purposes of:

(1) selecting a novel from a genre that they normally would not attempt in preparation for writing a novel review and

(2) selecting which center the group felt their "creation" was most successful in, polishing the work from that center, and sharing it with the class.

Center One: Science Fiction

Have the students read together what the characteristics of a science-fiction novel are.

As a group, have the students prepare a script for a scene for a new episode of *Star Trek*, taking something from science and adding the fiction to demonstrate the traits of science-fiction writing.

Rehearse. (If the students choose this as their center to present, they may wish to videotape the scene.)

Center Two: Mystery/Detective

Have the students read together the characteristics of this genre.

Using a selection of large art prints that depict crime or mystery (or prints within art books), have the students discuss at least five paintings by trying to decide what happened before the painting was painted and what happened afterward—looking for "clues" in the painting.

Have students select their favourite painting and prepare a five-scene tableaux (frozen stills) where as a group they reenact what happened before the painting, during the painting, afterward.

Center Three: Realistic Fiction

Have the students read together the characteristics of this genre.

Using copies of the daily newspaper, have the students scan the paper for three or four articles each that they feel could be turned into a successful realistic fiction novel.

As a group, have students decide on one article they agree has the most promise. Have each student write the opening paragraph(s) to this "new novel" and share it with the others to see how each writer interpreted the idea.

Center Four: Gothic Horror

Have the students read together the characteristics of this genre.

Have them tell each other the scariest ghost/horror story they can remember hearing from summer camp or other sources.

As a group, decide on one of the stories (most suited to a class presentation!). Have the group create a "gothic horror" rap of this story including sound effects. Rehearse. (If the students choose this as their center to present, they may wish to audiotape the rap.)

Center Five: Humor

Have the students read together the characteristics of this genre.

Have the students share with each other a humorous incident that they have been involved in.

From the four or five incidents shared, have the group choose one (suitable for sharing!) and create a comedic improvisation telling the story of the chosen incident.

Rehearse the scene.

Chapter 14

REFLECTIVE LEARNING

How do teacher-librarians assess—or, more important, reflect on—brain friendly school library learning experiences? How do they know that students have experienced success and "neural" growth results? Assessing brain friendly learning is much more complex than standard assessment tools might measure—paper tests, grades on research papers, and so on, give only some parts of measuring the learning landscape. The much bigger neural development concepts, those of becoming reflective learners and reflective practitioners, are not as easy to measure. Reflection is not a rushed process, nor a final one. It is ongoing and can be celebratory at the conclusion of a project or learning experience. It is something not done often enough, as curriculum units or library teaching projects are rushed through. Reflection in its variety of formats is something that the teacher-librarian and teacher planning teams need to strategically build into cooperative learning experiences in the school library.

Too often teacher-librarians find themselves rushed at the end of a large school library project, knowing that another "booking" begins the following week and hoping that any unfinished work or marking would be handled by the classroom teacher who would often grade the project and include it in the grade-term mark. What about the information literacy processes? Could the students transfer and apply them? Were the students thinking more deeply about their learning? What did they learn that was meaningful to them? What was meaningful about the project? The teacher and teacher librarian need to incorporate how they will partner for assessment and reflection, with the push to move into greater reflective practices around brain friendly school library experiences.

The emotional connection to learning is critical to patterning and long-term memory development. The emotional brain downshifts under "threatening" conditions, and for many students, these threatening conditions are tests. How different learning in schools would look if only traditional tests, grading, and grade levels could be eliminated and realistic project work, portfolios, and individual achievement could be reflected on radically different report cards. Is not this how most adult workers are assessed or evaluated in their careers? According to David Kolb (Kolb and Kolb 2001) and others who write about experiential learning, the brain needs ongoing feedback, rehearsal, and reflection to help learners understand how they are doing. Are they developing "habits of mind, heart and work?" What happens when no one is looking?

Strategies such as cooperative learning provide ongoing feedback from peer and teacher. Technology is a useful tool for immediate response. Checklists are useful for action research steps. Self-assessment is a major part of emotionally connecting to learning. Based on setting their own goals, students must be involved in creating rubrics with the teacher-librarian and teacher as part of the cooperative planning process. Rubrics can also facilitate safe and uncritical peer assessment and commentary about student work. When introducing a project such as making an alphabet book ("ABC Centers"), teacher-librarians can have the students discuss what would make an aesthetically pleasing alphabet book or letter. How would we know this is good work? It goes back to the importance of applying evaluative criteria to resources and to student work or works in progress.

Technology is also a useful tool for creating portfolios, another valuable way to reflect. Imagine students leaving a school system with a number of self-made CDs or DVDs containing what the students believed was their best work that year or in that division. Since many brain friendly school and school library projects will not be one-dimensional, the school library can be of great assistance (and provide leadership) in this area, as the library should contain the most up-to-date technologies for student use—scanners, cameras, CD burners, and so on. Keep the brain friendly school library Web page current and reflective of the ongoing library learning experience.

Celebration is an important aspect of reflective learning, a recognition of achievement. Celebration can take many forms—from daily observations made as students are working in the library to enjoying student "author posters" or other exhibits in a library "gallery" to holding a project fair or "character day" or other type of sharing or celebration event. Many schools conduct student-led parent-teacher conferences—the school library should be open during these times and the students invited to bring their parents in for an explanation of their current school library projects.

Journals are a popular tool for reflection, but they need to be considered very carefully in their use. Often journals, especially those used in reader's/writer's workshops, connect with school library programs such as "community of readers" and can quickly lose their "novelty" and become another dreaded exercise for many students rather than a tool for reflection and thinking. Guiding questions for journaling can appear to be or turn into another form of "worksheet" in many learners' minds. Students have groaned when they hear they are going to journal about a novel—could not they discuss it or act it out or just read it? And they have a point. Drawing, sketching, and mind mapping in journals push thinking to more sophisticated levels. Having students form their own questions helps slow their thinking down and presses toward greater reflective writing.

The students pose an interesting point when they say that instead of journaling or discussing, "couldn't they just read?" Reading is one of the ultimate forms of reflection, the relationship between the words on the page, the author, and the reader. Reading slows the mind down as it lets ideas and thoughts enter. It is unto itself a succinct, high-level activity and one for which schools often leave very little time. Educators "teach" reading and fret over readers who do not develop into good readers as early as they had like. They assign reading and book reports and imagine students spending hours at home pouring over a book. Some schools initiate programs like DEAR (Drop Everything and Read!) so that everyone must read at the same fifteen minutes or so each day. But what about time to "just read"?

Students need permission and time to just read. Some need to be read to, even at the high school level. Not everyone needs to read at the same time. The brain friendly library could facilitate "just reading areas"—from a comfortable chair surrounded by plants in a small elementary school library to a "coffee house" environment in a senior high with comfy chairs in quiet corners to table groupings with newspapers, water, perhaps even coffee to encourage light reading and discussion. When students are saying "let me *just* read," they are looking for that place to be in their often overplanned days to slow down, interact with the worlds of the imagination, and enjoy a good book. The following ideas focus on reflective practices around the concept of "just reading."

Primary: "How Does This Book Make Me Feel?"

- Pull a selection of current and classic picture books of varying levels and styles.

- Have the class scheduled into the library over four or five sessions, choose and trade books, and "just read." Some students may need to be read to or with. Have students make note of the titles and authors of favourite choices, focusing on how the books made them "feel." The teacher and teacher-librarian should expand on "feelings" vocabulary with word cards, introducing simple thesaurus, emotion lists, and so on.

- Have the students decide on their "top" favourite read that they will share with the class as a "book commercial." The commercial must run sixty seconds (practice with timers) and include title and author and five statements of feeling: "This book will make you feel joyous when Mudge gives Henry a big lick on the face." "It will make you feel frightened when Mudge gets lost." "It will make you feel hopeful when Mudge's paw prints are found." And so on.

• Videotape or have students learn to videotape—second and third graders really enjoy learning and using basic video skills. Celebrate with class, parents, or on the school library Web site.

Middle School: "Novel Reflections"

• Working with a teacher or group of same-grade teachers, team plan and share a "community of readers" group novel study project. Groups of four or five students choose a novel they wish to study together based on joint book talks given by the teacher-librarian and the teacher.

• Students select a first and second choice and can be grouped randomly based on choice or heterogeneously based on student need, benefits.

• For the first part of the project, let the students "just read." Some will finish quickly; other groups may need to be read to.

• Upon finishing the reading, have groups meet and dialogue to decide upon five key events from the novel that they felt on an emotional level. Some students will find this challenging and will need coaching from "I liked the book when . . ." to "I was terrified and disgusted when Jonas discovered what his father did when 'releasing' babies." Have a number of thesauruses available for the groups to develop emotional vocabulary further.

• Once students have identified key emotional scenes, ask them to decide how they wish to reflect upon one of these scenes from the novel using an artistic medium—visual art (painting, model, collage?), music (a soundtrack or rap song?), movement (choreograph a dance piece), or drama (skit, tableaux, monologue?). Choices may be dependent on talents of teachers involved and materials. That is, if students wish to create an emotional reflection of a novel's key scene in clay, there may not be access to a kiln, clay, and so on, or the teacher-librarian may need to involve the art teacher.

• The reflections can be put together as a gallery exhibition in the library (and on the school library Web page) with any drama/dance pieces shown on video stations and/or as an assembly with visual art shown on PowerPoint.

Secondary: "Emotions and Decisions"

• Have students choose an issue they currently feel strongly about—from weight loss to dating, global warming to parent pressure.

• Have them privately journal about the issue and brainstorm a number of decisions that could be considered around the issue.

• Assist them in choosing a novel that deals with a similar issue.

• Arrange "reading time" for the students, perhaps creating a "café" atmosphere (with student help) for this project if the school library environment is not already reflective of such an atmosphere.

• As the students read, have them add entries to their journal pertaining to how the novel is affecting their thinking on their issue/decisions.

• Have the students decide how they would like to share their reflections on the novels, with consideration for privacy. For example, they could create sophisticated advertisement posters for the library around "Decision Making Books" such as the ads in periodicals such as *Ad Busters*. The problems could be stated generically—for example, "How much weight to lose is too much?" "Is global warming real, or are they making it up?" "Parents are too strict."

REFERENCES

American Association of School Libraries. 1997. Information Literacy Standards for Student Learning. Available: http://www.ala.org/ala/aasl/aaslproftools/informationpower/informationliteracy.htm

American Library Association and the Association for Educational Communications and Technology. 1998. *Information Power: Building Partnerships for Learning.* Chicago: ALA.

Association for Teacher-Librarianship in Canada and the Canadian School Library Association. 1997. Students' Information Literacy Needs in the 21st Century: Competencies for Teacher-Librarians. Available: http://www.caslibraries.ca/publications/pub_literacy.aspx

Association for Teacher-Librarianship in Canada and the Canadian School Library Association. 2003. *Achieving Information Literacy: Standards for School Library Programs in Canada.* Chicago: ALA.

Brain Connection. 2004. Available: http://www.brainconnection.com

Brandt, Ron. 1997. On Using Knowledge about Our Brain: A Conversation with Bob Sylwester. *Educational Leadership* 54(6): 16–19.

Brown, Jean. 1997. Teacher-Librarians: Irrelevant Stage Managers or Pioneering Voyagers. Paper presented for Virtual Seminar I, Association for Teacher-Librarianship in Canada.

Caine, Renate Nummela, and Geoffrey Caine. 2004. Brain/Mind Learning. Available: http://www.cainelearning.com/brain

Caine, Renate Nummela, and Geoffrey Caine. 1997. *Education on the Edge of Possibility.* Alexandria, VA: ASCD.

Calgary Board of Education. 1991. *The Teacher-Librarian Resource Manual.* Calgary, Alberta, Canada: Calgary Board of Education.

Chepesiuk, R. 1996. Librarians as Cyberspace Guerrillas. *American Libraries* 27(8): 49–51.

Chudler, Eric H. Neuroscience for Kids. Available: http://faculty.washington.edu/chudler/cells.html

Cohen, Elizabeth G. 1994. *Designing Groupwork.* New York: Teachers College Press.

Creative Learning Systems. 2004. Available: http://www.clsinc.com

Dana Alliance for Brain Initiatives. 2004. Available: http://www.dana.org

Dickinson, Dee. 2004. New Horizons for Learning. Available: http://www.newhorizons.org

Ering, Timothy B. 2003. *The Story of Frog Belly Rat Bone.* Cambridge, MA: Candlewick Press.

Gardner, Howard. 1983. *Frames of Mind: The Theory of Multiple Intelligences.* New York: Basic Books.

Goleman, Daniel. 1995. *Emotional Intelligence: Why It Can Matter More Than IQ.* New York: Bantam.

Howard, Pierce J. 2000. *The Owner's Manual for the Brain.* 2nd ed. Atlanta, GA: Bard Press.

Jensen, Eric. 2004. Jensen Learning Corp. Available: http://jlcbrain.com/main.html

Jensen, Eric. 1996. *Brain-Based Learning.* Del Mar, CA: Turning Point.

Jensen, Eric. 1995. *The Learning Brain.* San Diego, CA: Turning Point.

Kagan, Spencer. 1990. The Structural Approach to Cooperative Learning. *Educational Leadership* 47(4): 12–15.

Kohn, Alfie. 1991, March. The Role of Schools. *Phi Delta Kappan.* May.

Kolb, A., and D. A. Kolb. 2001. *Experiential Learning Theory Bibliography 1971–2001.* Boston, MA: McBer. Available: http://www.infed.org/biblio/b-explrn.htm

Langer, Ellen J. 2005. http://www.wjh.harvard.edu/~langer

Langer, Ellen J. 1997. *The Power of Mindful Learning.* Reading, MA: Addison-Wesley.

Langford, Linda. 1998. Information Literacy: A Clarification. *School Libraries Worldwide* 4(1): 59–72.

McKenzie, Jamie. 1997. Deep Thinking and Deep Reading in an Age of Info-glut, Info-garbage, Info-glitz, and Info-gimmicks. Available: http://www.fromnowon.org

People for Education. 2004. The Arts in Ontario's Public Schools. Report by People for Education, Toronto, May.

San Diego University. 1998. The WebQuest Page. Available: http://webquest.sdsu.edu

Sprenger, Marilee. 1999. *Learning and Memory: The Brain in Action.* Alexandria, VA: ASCD.

Sykes, Judith. 2002. *Action Research—A Practical Guide to Transforming Your School Library.* Westport, CT: Libraries Unlimited.

Sykes, Judith. 1997. *Library Centers—Teaching Information Literacy, Skills, and Processes K–6.* Greenwood Village, CO: Libraries Unlimited.

Sylwester, Robert. 2005. Library Talk Columnists. http://www.brainconnection.com/library/?main-eduhome/teaching-brain

Slywester, Robert. 2004. *How to Explain a Brain: An Educator's Handbook of Brain Terms and Cognitive Processes.* Thousand Oaks, CA: Corwin Press.

Slywester, Robert. 2003. *A Biological Brain in a Cultural Classroom: Enhancing Cognitive and Social Development Through Collaborative Classroom Management.* 2nd ed. Thousand Oaks, CA: Corwin Press.

Sylwester, Robert. 2000. *A Biological Brain in a Cultural Classroom: Applying Biological Research to Classroom Management.* Thousand Oaks, CA: Corwin Press.

Sylwester, Robert. 1998. The Role of the Arts on Brain Development and Maintenance. Paper presented at the conference of the Alberta Association of Supervision and Curriculum Development, Calgary, Alberta, Canada, April.

Sylwester, Robert. 1995. *A Celebration of Neurons.* Alexandria, VA: ASCD.

Whole Brain Atlas. 2004. Available: http://www.med.harvard.edu/AANLIB/home
 .html

Wolfe, Pat. 2004. Mind Matters. Available: http://www.patwolfe.com

Wolfe, Pat. 2001. *Brain Matters: Translating Research into Classroom Practice*.
 Alexandria, VA: ASCD.

Wolfe, Pat. 1997. *Bringing Brain Research into Classroom Practice*. Salt Lake City,
 UT: Video Journal of Education. (video recording)

Wolfe, Patricia, and Pamela Nevills. 2004. *Building the Reading Brain, PreK–3*.
 Thousand Oaks, CA: Corwin Press.

INDEX

About the Author

JUDITH ANNE SYKES has gone from a junior high school language arts/drama teacher, an elementary teacher-librarian, to School Library Specialist for the Calgary Board of Education, Assistant Principal, and Principal. Judith consults, makes educational presentations, and has extensively published locally, provincially, nationally, and internationally including being editor of IMPACT, the professional journal of the Association of Teacher-Librarianship of Canada. She is the author of *Library Centers: Teaching Information Literacy, Skills, and Processes K–6* and *Action Research: Practical Tips for Transforming Your School Library.*